Contents

100 Literacy Assessment Lessons: Year 2

'Assessment' refers to all those activities undertaken by teachers, and by their students in assessing themselves, which provide information to be used as feedback to modify the teaching and learning activities in which they are engaged.'

from Black and William *Inside the Black Box*

About the series

100 Literacy Assessment Lessons is a response to the Assessment for Learning strategy (AfL) and Assessing Pupils' Progress (APP) and contains all new, stand-alone material. The lessons mirror the guidelines and viewpoints of the revised approach to assessment. The CD-ROMs provide appropriate and exciting texts and a variety of assessment activities from photocopiable pages for individual, whole-class or group work to stimulating interactive activities. Together, the books and CD-ROMs will be an invaluable resource to help you understand and implement the revised approach to assessment.

About assessment

The key points of the revised approach to assessment are as follows:
- Assessments are accurate and linked to National Curriculum levels;
- Assessments are targeted, with assessment focuses used as the guiding criteria;
- Assessments are reliable and based on a range of evidence;
- Assessments are useful and appropriate: day to day, periodic or transitional.

Type of assessment	Purpose	Strategies
Day to day	Ongoing and formative: encourages reflection and informs the next steps in teaching and learning.	Objectives, outcomes and success criteria are made explicit and are shared with children; observations are used to gather evidence; peer assessment and self-assessment help to develop children as responsible learners.
Periodic	Provides a periodic view of children's progress and diagnostic information linked to national standards.	Progress and attainment are reviewed regularly (half-termly or termly) against APP criteria; strengths and gaps in learning are identified to inform future planning.
Transitional	Brings together evidence, including tests, at points of transition (eg level to level or year to year); provides a formal overview of children's attainment set within the framework of national standards.	Use of formal tasks and tests; external validation and reporting.

For a complete list of strategies for day-to-day assessment and further information about periodic and transitional assessment, visit the National Strategies website (**http://nationalstrategies.standards.dcsf.gov.uk**).

What are assessment focuses (AFs)?

Assessment focuses (AFs) are tools for assessment that sit between the National Curriculum programmes of study and level descriptions. The AFs provide more detailed criteria against which children's standards of attainment can be assessed and judged.

About the book
Reflecting the structure of the renewed Primary Framework for Literacy (2006), the book is divided into three Blocks: Narrative, Non-fiction and Poetry. Each Block is further divided into Units, and the Units are split into Phases. The Phases are divided into a number of day-to-day assessment activities. These assessment activities, based on learning outcomes, are designed to fit easily into your existing planning.

Units
Each Unit covers a different text type or genre and, because of this, each Unit has its own introduction containing the following:
Literacy objectives: All objectives for the Unit are listed under their strand names.
Key aspects of learning: Aspects of learning that the Unit covers are identified from the renewed Primary National Strategy (PNS) Framework.
Assessment focuses (AFs): The main assessment focuses that are addressed during the Unit are listed from APP.
Speaking and listening: Assessment areas you should look out for are linked to the Speaking and listening strand objectives.
Resources: Lists all of the resources required for the activities in each Phase.
Planning grids: There are two grids per Unit to provide an overview of the Unit and to suggest how you can build assessment opportunities into your medium-term planning. The grids show Phases, learning outcomes, a summary of lessons, assessment opportunities and potential evidence, levelled statements of the assessment focuses (AFs), and success criteria matched to the learning outcomes in the form of 'I can...' statements.

Assessment activities
Each assessment activity follows the same format:
Learning outcomes: These are relevant to individual activities or a set of activities that share objectives.
Success criteria: These are child-friendly 'I can...' statements for children or teachers to refer to during or following the activity.
Setting the context: This section provides guidance on what the task is and details the children's expected prior learning. The context for the task may also be explained: group, paired or individual work. Where adult support is required, this is also described.
Assessment opportunity: This section highlights what to assess, how to find out what children know, and what questions to ask.
Assessment evidence: This section suggests what to look for during an activity in relation to specific assessment focuses (AFs).
Next steps: This section is divided into support and extension. It provides ideas to enable children to revisit an objective or learning outcome, and gives feedback or targets to move children forward, consolidate or extend their learning.
Key aspects of learning: Key aspects of learning are linked to specific activities.

Photocopiable pages
At the end of each Unit is a selection of photocopiable activity pages. The full range of these is provided on the CD-ROM, including levelled versions where appropriate. Photocopiable pages may include self-assessment statements for ticking as well as a 'traffic light' system for colouring (see 'Self-assessment' on page 7 for more information.) Where 'I can...' statements are not included, peer assessment may be suggested within an activity.

Transitional assessment
Also included on the CD-ROM are some SATs-style formal single-level assessments. More information about these can be found on page 7, and a grid detailing their content is provided on page 174.

How to use the materials

The activities in the book provide a balance of whole-class/group/paired/ independent learning and teaching, and give the opportunity not only for day-to-day assessment but also for collection of evidence against individual assessment focuses (AFs) for periodic review. Each activity can be slotted into a lesson where appropriate and may involve discussion work, written responses, use of photocopiable pages or interactive activities.

Two periodic assessment activities are provided at the end of each Unit – one for reading and one for writing. The focus of each of these activities is usually a photocopiable page that assesses children on the learning outcomes covered during the Unit and provides further evidence against the assessment focuses. You can also use these periodic assessments to help you to make level judgements that match to the Reading and Writing Attainment Targets (ATs).

Making a level judgement

Assessment involves making a level judgement against national standards at regular intervals. The following steps will support you in adopting a strategic approach to the marking and levelling needed for assessment.

Step one: Consider evidence
- Use a range of appropriate evidence to make a level judgement, for example, written or oral;
- Remember that it is quality not quantity that matters;
- Keep examples of children's work that will provide significant evidence.

Step two: Review the evidence
- Take a broader view of a child's achievement across the whole subject and over time;
- Create a visual picture of strengths and learning gaps by highlighting criteria a child has met across a range of evidence;
- Collaborate with colleagues and agree what constitutes success for the various assessment criteria.

Step three: Make a judgement
- Consult the English Assessment Guidelines (see National Standards website: **http://nationalstrategies.standards.dcsf.gov.uk** and look at exemplar material provided in the Standards files;
- Arrive at an overall subject level judgement;
- Think about what the child demonstrates:
  - How much of the level;
  - How consistently;
  - How independently;
  - In what range of contexts.
- Finally, fine-tune your levelling to 'high', 'secure' or 'low'.

What's on the CD-ROM?

Each CD-ROM contains a wealth of resources. These include:
- **Photocopiable pages:** levelled where appropriate, including text extracts and activity sheets for day-to-day and periodic assessment.
- **Transitional assessments:** single-level tests for levels 1–3 including mark schemes and instructions.
- **Interactive activities:** for individuals or small groups, with in-built marking to assess specific learning outcomes.
- **Whiteboard tools:** a set of tools (including a pen, highlighter, eraser, notes and reward stickers) that can be used to annotate activity sheets or interactive activities. These tools will work on any interactive whiteboard or conventional screen.
- **Editable planning grids** (in Word format) are available to help teachers integrate the assessment activities into their medium-term and weekly planning.

How to use the CD-ROM

System requirements
Minimum specification:
- PC or Mac with a CD-ROM drive and 512 Mb RAM (recommended)
- Windows 2000 or above/Mac OSX version 10.4 or above
- Recommended minimum processor speed: 1 GHz

Getting started
The *100 Literacy Assessment Lessons* CD-ROM should auto run when inserted into your CD drive. If it does not, browse to your CD drive to view the contents of the CD-ROM and click on the *100 Literacy Assessment Lessons* icon.

From the start-up screen you will find four options: select **Credits** to view a list of acknowledgements. Click on **Register** to register the product in order to receive product updates and special offers. Click on **How to use this CD-ROM** to access support notes for using the CD-ROM. Finally, if you agree to the terms and conditions, select **Start** to move to the main menu.

For all technical support queries, contact Scholastic Customer Services help desk on 0845 6039091.

Navigating the CD-ROM
The CD-ROM allows users to search for resources by Block or Unit, or by assessment focus. Users can also search by assessment type (day to day, periodic or transitional) or by resource type (for example, worksheet, interactive resource, or text extract).

Day-to-day assessments
These should be used to support learning. They can be used during a lesson, when you judge that children are ready for an assessment activity. The materials can also be used weekly or after a unit of work has been completed.

Periodic assessments
These can be used with a group of children rather than with the whole class. This could be at the end of a unit of work (for example, at the end of a half-term or term). Decide who is ready to be assessed using the outcomes of the day-to-day assessment activities and your observations of children's performance.

Self-assessment
There is a 'traffic light' system at the bottom of some photocopiable pages that children can shade to show how they feel about the activity: red for 'need help'; orange for 'having some understanding'; green for 'I found this easy!'. (Alternatively, you may wish to utilise these as a teacher marking tool for providing an at-a-glance guide to the child's progress.)

The photocopiable sheets also provide 'I can...' statements with tick boxes, to enable children to self-assess specifically in terms of the relevant learning outcomes/success criteria. A similar system is in place at the end of all the interactive activities, where the children are asked to click on a traffic light, and to type in any comments.

Transitional tests
These single-level tests provide evidence of where, in relation to national standards, children are at a given point in time. There are two Reading and Writing assessments for each level. Each reading assessment consists of a two-part reading comprehension test based on two different text types. Each writing assessment consists of two writing tasks – shorter and longer – that focus on writing for different purposes. All the tasks and tests for levels 1-3 are included on the CD-ROM together with easy-to-follow marking schemes (see pages 174–175 for more information.)

Class PET
A whole-school version of *100 Literacy Assessment Lessons* is available with an expanded range of digital assessment activities, as well as the facility to report, record and track children's work. For further information visit the Class PET website, **www.scholastic.co.uk/classpet**.

Periodic assessment

Unit	AT	Page	Assessment focuses	Learning outcomes
Narrative 1	Reading	20	AF2, AF4	Children can sequence the different parts of a story. Children understand story structure and the use of temporal connectives.
	Writing	20	AF3, AF4, AF7	Children can write notes and use them to write a story. Children can understand story structure and the use of temporal connectives.
Narrative 2	Reading	34	AF1, AF2, AF5	Children can express ideas about a character using evidence from the text. Children understand that connectives can be used to link ideas and create tension in narrative.
	Writing	35	AF3, AF4, AF7	Children can understand that text must match character action. Children can identify and add connectives.
Narrative 3	Reading	49	AF2, AF3, AF5, AF6	Children can talk about a text and explain their reaction to it. Children can make inferences about characters and use the text to support their answers.
	Writing	50	AF1, AF2, AF3, AF7, AF8	Children can plan and write a sustained story about a familiar character. Children can use the past tense, third person and can include some dialogue and detail to add interest.
Narrative 4	Reading	64	AF2, AF3, AF6	Children can plan a story that has a logical sequence of events. Children can work as a member of a group to present a scene from a known story to an audience. .
	Writing	65	AF1, AF3, AF7, AF8	Children can plan a story that has a logical sequence of events. Children can write an extended narrative with: a logical sequence of events; sentences grouped together; temporal connectives; consistent use of the third person and past tense.
Non-fiction 1	Reading	79	AF4, AF5	Children can read and follow a simple sequence of instructions related to another curriculum area or classroom procedure.
	Writing	80	AF2, AF3, AF7	Children can write a simple sequence of instructions to be followed by another child or group.

📖 Periodic assessment

Unit	AT	Page	Assessment focuses	Learning outcomes
Non-fiction 2	Reading	93	AF1, AF2, AF4, AF6	Children demonstrate that they have understood information read from a book or screen by noting the main points. Children can make choices about the best way to present information in an explanation text, using flow charts and diagrams.
	Writing	94	AF2, AF3, AF7	Children can note information collected from more than one source. Children can construct a pictorial flow chart. Children can write and evaluate explanation texts.
Non-fiction 3	Reading	108	AF1, AF2	Children can do research and make notes from books and ICT texts. Children can compare and evaluate research material.
	Writing	109	AF1, AF2	Children can use their notes to write a simple information text. Children can complete and evaluate a simple information text.
Non-fiction 4	Reading	123	AF2, AF4	Children can identify and evaluate non-chronological reports, using the text layout features to find information.
	Writing	124	AF4, AF7	Children can write a non-chronological report on a theme, using subheadings, key details and information to structure the text. Children can evaluate non-chronological reports, expressing their views clearly and using evidence from the text.
Poetry 1	Reading	138	AF1, AF3, AF4, AF5	Children can listen to, read and perform poems, identifying different patterns in their language use and structure.
	Writing	139	AF1, AF2, AF7	Children can write a simple poem of their own, playing with interesting and inventive language choices to create or continue a particular pattern.
Poetry 2	Reading	153	AF1, AF2, AF3	Children can recognise the careful selection of words.
	Writing	154	AF1, AF2, AF7	Children can write a simple poem of their own in response to direct observation.
Poetry 3	Reading	168	AF3, AF5, AF6	Children can recognise how language choices can make a poem seem funny.
	Writing	169	AF2, AF7	Children can write a simple poem of their own, playing with interesting and inventive language choices to create or continue a particular pattern.

NARRATIVE

UNIT 1 Stories with familiar settings

Literacy objectives

Speak and listen for a wide range of purposes in different contexts

Strand 1 Speaking
- Tell real and imagined stories using the conventions of familiar story language.

Strand 2 Listening and responding
- Respond to presentations by describing characters, repeating some highlights and commenting constructively.

Strand 4 Drama
- Present part of traditional stories, their own stories or work drawn from different parts of the curriculum for members of their own class.

Read and write for a range of purposes on paper and on screen

Strand 5 Word recognition: decoding (reading) and encoding (spelling)
- Read independently and with increasing fluency longer and less familiar texts.
- Read high and medium frequency words independently and automatically.

Strand 6 Word structure and spelling
- Spell with increasing accuracy and confidence, drawing on word recognition and knowledge of word structure, and spelling patterns including common inflections and use of double letters.
- Read and spell less common alternative graphemes including trigraphs.

Strand 7 Understanding and interpreting texts
- Draw together ideas and information from across a whole text, using simple signposts in the text.
- Give some reasons why things happen or characters change.

Strand 8 Engaging with and responding to texts
- Engage with books through exploring and enacting interpretations.
- Explain their reactions to texts, commenting on important aspects.

Strand 9 Creating and shaping texts
- Draw on knowledge and experience of texts in deciding and planning what and how to write.
- Select from different presentational features to suit particular writing purposes on paper and on screen.

Strand 10 Text structure and organisation
- Use planning to establish clear sections for writing.
- Use appropriate language to make sections hang together.

Strand 11 Sentence structure and punctuation
- Write simple and compound sentences and begin to use subordination in relation to time and reason.

Key aspects of learning

Problem solving
● Children will respond to a task using trial and error and consider a range of possible solutions.

Creative thinking
● Children will generate imaginative ideas to make connections and see relationships between different modes of communication. Children will experiment with different modes of communication to respond to different points of view.

Evaluation
● Children will discuss success criteria for their written and oral work, give feedback to others and judge the effectiveness of their own writing and speaking.

Social skills
● When working collaboratively, children will learn about listening to and respecting other people's ideas and taking on different roles within a group.

Assessment focuses

Reading
AF2 (understand, describe, select or retrieve information, events or ideas from texts and use quotation and reference to text).
AF3 (deduce, infer or interpret information, events or ideas from texts).

Writing
AF3 (organise and present whole texts effectively, sequencing and structuring information, ideas and events).

Speaking and listening
Speaking (speak with clarity and use intonation).
Listening and responding (listen with sustained concentration).
Drama (improvise and sustain roles).

Resources

Phase 1 activities
Photocopiable page, 'Lost!'
Interactive activity, 'Sequencing'
Photocopiable page, 'Picture plan'
Phase 2 activities
Photocopiable page, 'Being different'
Photocopiable page, 'What I think'
Phase 3 activities
Photocopiable page, 'Lost!'
Photocopiable page, 'Character storyline'
Photocopiable page, 'Being different'
Photocopiable page, 'Story planner'
Periodic assessment
Photocopiable page, 'Narrative 1 Reading assessment text'
Photocopiable page, 'Narrative 1 Reading assessment'
Photocopiable page, 'Narrative 1 Writing assessment'

Unit 1 📖 Stories with familiar settings

Learning outcomes	Assessment opportunity and evidence	Assessment focuses (AFs)	Success criteria
		Level 1	
Phase ① activities pages 15-16			
Sequencing Children can sequence the main parts of a story.	• Paired activity where children discuss the story 'Lost!', complete the interactive sequencing activity and use pictures to prompt their retelling of the story. • Children's discussion and completion of the interactive sequencing activity, oral responses and retelling of the story.	**Reading AF2** • Some simple points from familiar texts recalled. • Some pages/sections of interest located.	I can sequence the main parts of a story.
Storytelling Children can plan and sequence pictorially a story.	• Paired activity where children share ideas for a setting for a new story about the boy from 'Lost!' and plan and sequence their stories on a storyboard. • Children's group discussion and completed storyboards.	**Writing AF3** • Some formulaic phrases indicate start/end of text. • Events/ideas sometimes in appropriate order.	I can plan a story in pictures.
Phase ② activities pages 17-18			
Character viewpoints Children can understand that characters have different points of view.	• Paired activity where children listen to a reading of 'Being different' and role play the main characters before completing the photocopiable page. • Children's discussion, role play and written responses on the photocopiable.	**Reading AF3** • Reasonable inference at a basic level. • Comments/questions about meaning of parts of text.	I can understand that characters have different points of view.
Character actions Children can understand that characters could follow different courses of action.	• Paired activity, where children listen to a rereading of 'Being different', consider the actions of the main characters and plan and role play new character actions. • Children's group discussion and presentation of their new story.	**Reading AF3** • Reasonable inference at a basic level. • Comments/questions about meaning of parts of text.	I can understand that characters could follow different courses of action.
Phase ③ activities pages 18-19			
Story structure Children can describe what a character does in a story.	• Paired activity where children discuss the characters and key actions from the story 'Lost!' and complete a pictorial storyline, charting the main character's key actions. • Children's discussion of the characters and completed pictorial storyboards.	**Writing AF3** • Some formulaic phrases indicate start/end of text. • Events/ideas sometimes in appropriate order.	I can show a character's storyline in pictures.

Unit 1 Stories with familiar settings

Learning outcomes	Assessment opportunity and evidence	Assessment focuses (AFs)	Success criteria
		Level 1	
Story planning Children can use the *opening - something happens - events to sort it out - ending* structure to plan a story.	● Paired activity where children label their previous story plans with stage headings and then add written notes using the photocopiable page. ● Children's discussion of storyboards, labelling of stories and written notes on the photocopiable.	**Writing AF3** ● Some formulaic phrases indicate start/end of text. ● Events/ideas sometimes in appropriate order.	I can write notes to plan a story.

Learning outcomes	Assessment opportunity and evidence	Assessment focuses (AFs)		Success criteria
		Level 2	Level 3	
Phase 1 activities pages 15–16				
Sequencing Children can sequence the main parts of a story.	● Paired activity where children discuss the story 'Lost!', complete the interactive sequencing activity and use pictures to prompt their retelling of the story. ● Children's discussion and completion of the interactive sequencing activity, oral responses and retelling of the story.	**Reading AF2** ● Some specific straightforward information recalled. ● Generally clear idea of where to look for information.	**Reading AF2** ● Simple, most obvious points identified though there may also be some misunderstanding. ● Some comments include quotations from or references to text, but not always relevant.	I can sequence the main parts of a story.
Storytelling Children can plan and sequence pictorially a story.	● Paired activity where children share ideas for a setting for a new story about the boy from 'Lost!' and plan and sequence their stories on a storyboard. ● Children's group discussion and completed storyboards.	**Writing AF3** ● Some basic sequencing of ideas or material. ● Openings and/or closings sometimes signalled.	**Writing AF3** ● Some attempt to organise ideas with related points placed next to each other. ● Openings and closings usually signalled. ● Some attempt to sequence ideas or material logically.	I can plan a story in pictures.
Phase 2 activities pages 17–18				
Character viewpoints Children can understand that characters have different points of view.	● Paired activity where children listen to a reading of 'Being different' and role play the main characters before completing the photocopiable page. ● Children's discussion, role play and written responses on the photocopiable.	**Reading AF3** ● Simple, plausible inference about events and information, using evidence from text. ● Comments based on textual cues, sometimes misunderstood.	**Reading AF3** ● Straightforward inference based on a single point of reference in the text. ● Responses to text show meaning established at a literal level or based on personal speculation.	I can understand that characters have different points of view.

Unit 1 ▢ Stories with familiar settings

Learning outcomes	Assessment opportunity and evidence	Assessment focuses (AFs)		Success criteria
		Level 2	Level 3	
Character actions Children can understand that characters could follow different courses of action.	● Paired activity, where children listen to a rereading of 'Being different', consider the actions of the main characters and plan and role play new character actions. ● Children's group discussion and presentation of their new story.	**Reading AF3** ● Simple, plausible inference about events and information, using evidence from text. ● Comments based on textual cues, sometimes misunderstood.	**Reading AF3** ● Straightforward inference based on a single point of reference in the text. ● Responses to text show meaning established at a literal level or based on personal speculation.	I can understand that characters could follow different courses of action.
Phase ③ activities pages 18–19				
Story structure Children can describe what a character does in a story.	● Paired activity where children discuss the characters and key actions from the story 'Lost!' and complete a pictorial storyline, charting the main character's key actions. ● Children's discussion of the characters and completed pictorial storyboards.	**Writing AF3** ● Some basic sequencing of ideas or material. ● Openings and/or closings sometimes signalled.	**Writing AF3** ● Some attempt to organise ideas with related points placed next to each other. ● Openings and closings usually signalled. ● Some attempt to sequence ideas or material logically.	I can show a character's storyline in pictures.
Story planning Children can use the *opening - something happens - events to sort it out - ending* structure to plan a story.	● Paired activity where children label their previous story plans with stage headings and then add written notes using the photocopiable page. ● Children's discussion of storyboards, labelling of stories and written notes on the photocopiable.	**Writing AF3** ● Some basic sequencing of ideas or material. ● Openings and/or closings sometimes signalled.	**Writing AF3** ● Some attempt to organise ideas with related points placed next to each other. ● Openings and closings usually signalled. ● Some attempt to sequence ideas or material logically.	I can write notes to plan a story.

Phase ① Sequencing

Learning outcome
Children can sequence the main parts of a story.

Success criteria
I can sequence the main parts of a story.

Setting the context
Prior to this assessment, the children will need to have read, listened to and told stories. They should recognise that a story has different parts and have experience of sequencing them. Read aloud the story, 'Lost!' from the photocopiable page. Allow time for the children to discuss the story before introducing the interactive activity.

Assessment opportunity
Ask the children to work in pairs to complete the first screen of the interactive activity 'Sequencing'. The children must place the images in the sequence that they occurred in the story. Once the children are happy with their choices, print out each pair's results. In pairs, invite the children to take turns playing the roles of storyteller and listener. The storyteller should retell the story to their listener, using the printed screen of pictures from the interactive activity as a prompt. Afterwards, let pairs progress to the second screen of the activity to assess if they can sequence a written version of the story.

Assessment evidence
At level 1, the children should understand the main sequence of the story and cope with the first screen of the interactive activity. When retelling the story to their partner, they will sometimes need to return to an earlier section having overlooked important details. At levels 2–3, the children will sequence events more confidently and may identify and correct an error in their picture sequencing when retelling the story. This activity will provide evidence towards Reading AF2.

Next steps
Support: If the children find the interactive sequencing difficult, reduce the task so that the children are just looking for the beginning and ending of the story. Once these have been determined, they can then add the remaining story sections. If children struggle with oral storytelling, let partners help each other out.
Extension: Print a copy of the second screen from the interactive activity so that children can do their own checking as they compare it with their picture sequence. Challenge them to add an event to each page.

Key aspects of learning
Problem solving: Children will respond to a task using trial and error and consider a range of possible solutions.

Phase ① Storytelling

Learning outcome
Children can plan and sequence pictorially a story.

Success criteria
I can plan a story in pictures.

Setting the context
The children will need to have completed the previous activity and sequenced a story. Display an enlarged copy of the photocopiable page 'Picture plan'. Retell, in your own words, key events from the story 'Lost!' using the four images as a prompt. Explain to the children that they are going to create a new story featuring Carl. Discuss some familiar settings where this new story could take place, such as a school, a supermarket, a park or the beach.

Assessment opportunity

In pairs, ask the children to think about and discuss a new adventure for Carl. Then, give each child a sheet of paper with four numbered boxes on it. Invite them to use the boxes to create a pictorial storyboard. Remind them that they should be using their storyboard to show the key events of their story, ordering these in the sequence that they take place. Afterwards, put the children into small groups to share their stories, using their pictures as verbal prompts.

Assessment evidence

At level 1, the children will create a simple pictorial story with a beginning and an ending and will tell it simply. At levels 2-3, the children will create more complicated stories with most of the pictures sequenced logically. They will be more capable at storytelling, keeping their listeners' attention by making good use of their voice and facial expressions. This activity will provide evidence towards Writing AF3.

Next steps

Support: If the children struggle for story ideas, help with suggestions. For example, Jaye's doll could go missing or Carl could catch chickenpox.
Extension: Suggest the children use the 'three stars and a wish' technique to evaluate another child's storytelling. They identify three reasons why the storytelling was effective, and then suggest one area for improvement.

Key aspects of learning

Creative thinking: Children will generate imaginative ideas to make connections and see relationships between different modes of communication. Children will experiment with different modes of communication to respond to different points of view.
Evaluation: Children will discuss success criteria for their written and oral work, give feedback to others and judge the effectiveness of their own writing and speaking.

Phase ② Character viewpoints

Learning outcome
Children can understand that characters have different points of view.

Success criteria

I can understand that characters have different points of view.

Setting the context

Prior to this assessment, the children will need to understand that characters differ and are key elements of a story. They should also have experience of role play. Read the story 'Being different' from the photocopiable page. Explain to the children that they are going to explore the two main characters in the story – Arthur and William.

Assessment opportunity

Put the children into pairs, one to be William and one to be Arthur. Using role play, invite them to talk to each other about playtime at school, and how they feel about it. Remind them to focus on their character's point of view rather than their own. Once the children have role-played their character, give them the photocopiable page 'What I think' to record the thoughts and feelings of both characters.

Assessment evidence

At level 1, the children will recognise that the characters have different views. They may need prompting to stay in role. At levels 2-3, the children's dramatic interpretations are likely to be based on a single event in the story and they will be more consistent in their role play use of 'I'. This activity will provide evidence towards Reading AF3.

Next steps

Support: If the children struggle with role play, assess their understanding of the characters' viewpoints by oral questioning.
Extension: Ask the children to do a similar role play using the characters of William and Mum, exploring what would have happened when William returned home that day.

Key aspects of learning

Creative thinking: Children will generate imaginative ideas to make connections and see relationships between different modes of communication. Children will experiment with different modes of communication to respond to different points of view.
Social skills: When working collaboratively, children will learn about listening to and respecting other people's ideas and taking on different roles within a group.

Phase ② Character actions

Learning outcome
Children can understand that characters could follow different courses of action.

Success criteria
I can understand that characters could follow different courses of action.

Setting the context
The children should understand that stories have different key events and characters. They should have experience of making reference to characters and their actions and have already completed the previous activity. Re-read the story 'Being different' from the photocopiable page. Remind the children of their work in the previous activity, revisiting the characters of William and Arthur and their thoughts regarding playtime.

Assessment opportunity
Put the children into the same pairs as before. Ask partners to plan new courses of action for the two characters, William and Arthur. Encourage partner discussion and rehearsal before the children present their new version of the story. Ask individuals to retell, in role, the new events from their character's point of view.

Assessment evidence
At level 1, the children will recognise characters can behave differently. They may benefit from some suggested alternative actions. At levels 2–3, the children will be able to work independently and will recognise that they are making the story change. Their role plays may be based on their own personal feelings instead of the feeling of the characters in the text. This activity will provide evidence towards Reading AF3.

Next steps
Support: Offer support with a list of possible actions for William and Arthur. Let partners work together on new actions for just one of the characters.
Extension: Extend the task to Mum and William's actions after school that day.

Key aspects of learning
Social skills: When working collaboratively, children will learn about listening to and respecting other people's ideas and taking on different roles within a group.

NARRATIVE

Phase ③ Story structure

Learning outcome
Children can describe what a character does in a story.

Success criteria
I can show a character's storyline in pictures.

Setting the context
Carry out this assessment once the children have discussed characters from a range stories and have commented on their actions. They should also know that it is the character's actions that create a storyline. Re-read to the whole class the story 'Lost!' from the photocopiable page. Put the children into pairs to discuss the characters and the key actions that they take.

Assessment opportunity
Listen to the partner discussions in order to observe the children's grasp of the character actions. Then, provide the children with copies of the photocopiable page 'Character storyline' to record, pictorially and in sequence, important actions taken by Carl. At levels 2-3, the children should also be encouraged to add a sentence to each of their pictures, describing the key action. Assess whether the children are able to sequence and structure effectively their pictures and writing, on the photocopiable page .

Assessment evidence
At level 1, the children will record Carl's actions pictorially and they will be able to add some captions, with support. Their pictures and captions may tend to focus on Carl's actions from the beginning and the ending of the story. At levels 2-3, the children will be able to add writing to their pictures, describing the key actions and they will attempt to sequence the material logically. They may also use some time-related vocabulary, such as 'then', 'next' or 'after that', in their writing. This activity will provide evidence towards Writing AF3.

Next steps
Support: If the picture sequence is wrong, discuss the children's pictures with them to see if they can reorder them. Consider asking the children to draw pictures on separate pieces of paper, sequencing them and then sticking them in the boxes on the photocopiable page.
Extension: Ask the children to think about which of the four actions has most effect on the story's plot.

Key aspects of learning
Problem solving: Children will respond to a task using trial and error and consider a range of possible solutions.
Social skills: When working collaboratively, children will learn about listening to and respecting other people's ideas and taking on different roles within a group.

Phase ③ Story planning

Learning outcome
Children can use the *opening - something happens - events to sort it out - ending* structure to plan a story.

Success criteria
I can write notes to plan a story.

Setting the context
The children should understand the need for a story structure and be familiar with the terms: 'opening', 'something happens', 'events to sort it out', 'ending'. They should have collaborated as a class on planning a story and know how to write notes. Remind the children of the story 'Being different' from the photocopiable page. Give the children their pictorial storyboards from the Phase 1 activity, 'Storytelling'. Ask them to use the images to retell their story to a partner, swapping roles afterwards.

Assessment opportunity
Explain to the children that they are going to be writing up their new stories about Carl. Before they can do that, they must ensure that they have planned their story properly. Talk about the *opening - something happens - events to sort it out - ending* structure. Give four labels to every child, with each label displaying one of these headings. Ask them to place each label above the appropriate storyboard box on their sheet, sticking them down once correct. Suggest that they will also need written notes in order to write their story. Give everyone the photocopiable page 'Story planner' to write notes, matching their pictorial storyboard. Remind the children that these are just notes and can comprise simple words and phrases rather than full sentences. When the children place the story labels, assess and record their grasp of sequential story structure by observing if they position them correctly.

Assessment evidence
At level 1, the children will only write brief notes on their story planner and their writing may tend to signal only the opening and the closing of the story. At levels 2–3, the children's notes should include more detail. This activity will provide evidence towards Writing AF3.

Next steps
Support: Help the children who are less-confident writers by scribing some very brief story planner notes. They may also benefit from the use of story props to retell all four stages of the story
Extension: Suggest the children use the 'Story planner' to note useful time connectives that they could use at each stage of their story.

Key aspects of learning
Creative thinking: Children will generate imaginative ideas to make connections and see relationships between different modes of communication. Children will experiment with different modes of communication to respond to different points of view.

NARRATIVE

Periodic assessment

Reading

Learning outcomes
- Children can sequence the different parts of a story.
- Children understand story structure and the use of temporal connectives.

Success criteria
- I can sequence the main parts of a story.
- I can find time connectives in a story.

Setting the context
Tell the children that you are going to read them a new story, pausing after each paragraph for them to draw what has just happened in the correct box.

Assessment opportunity
Give each child a sheet of paper divided into four boxes. Ask them to number the boxes from one to four. Read aloud 'The safari park' from the photocopiable page 'Narrative 1 Reading assessment text'. Pause after each paragraph, so the children can sketch what has happened. Afterwards, give the children copies of the photocopiable page 'Narrative 1 Reading assessment'. Ask them to cut out the four sections and put them in order.

Assessment evidence
All of the children should show important information from the relevant sections of the story in their drawings. At levels 2–3, the children should cope more quickly with ordering the muddled story and should identify time connectives. This activity will provide evidence for Reading AF2 and AF4 and will help you judge the children's overall level in Reading.

Writing

Learning outcomes
- Children can write notes and use them to write a story.
- Children can understand story structure and the use of temporal connectives.

Success criteria
- I can use notes to write a story.
- I can use time connectives in a story.

Setting the context
Remind the children that they have planned their own story on a pictorial storyboard and written notes on a story planner (see Phase 1 activity, 'Storytelling' and Phase 3 activity, 'Story planning'). Revise the use of time connectives and display a class collection.

Assessment opportunity
Let the children use their storyboards to retell their story to a partner, and then look at their notes before starting their written version. Allow ample writing time, emphasising the benefit of rehearsing sentences mentally before writing them down. Afterwards, give them the photocopiable page 'Narrative 1 Writing assessment' for them to complete independently.

Assessment evidence
At level 1, the children will need reminders to use their storyboards and notes as a guide. They will follow the basic structure of their planned story, but may forget to include some detail. They will need to be encouraged to look for places to add suggested time connectives. At levels 2–3, the children will make good use of their pictorial and written plans, and may deviate from them as they recognise that improvements can be made. They will use some time connectives. This activity will provide evidence against Writing AF3, AF4 and AF7 and will help you judge the children's overall level in Writing.

Lost!

Carl was busy in his living room at home. He was doing important homework: making a model of his house for tomorrow's whole-school assembly. He looked carefully at a photograph Mum had given him. First, he checked that the details of his model matched the front of his real house. Then, he added the final piece:

a chimney pot.

"Finished!" he exclaimed.

"Hat," said his baby sister, sitting on the floor, playing with her doll.

"Not hat, house!" emphasised Carl.

Afterwards, Carl wandered off to the kitchen to help Mum.

"I wish Jaye would talk sense," he grumbled.

"She does talk some sense," replied Mum.

"More like nonsense!" said Carl. "Fancy forgetting 'house'!" Then, Carl laid the table while Mum made soup and toast. After that, she collected Jaye and sat her in her chair. Finally, they ate.

After tea, they went to look at the model.

"Magnificent!" exclaimed Mum. At first, Carl beamed proudly; then he noticed something.

"The chimney pot!" he gasped. "I know I stuck it on! It's gone!" Immediately, Carl and Mum hunted everywhere – on tables, under chairs, under cushions and on the floor. Carl moved Jaye's toys, and then he spotted... the chimney pot on a doll's head!

"Jaye thought it was a hat!" laughed Mum.

"Maybe she talks sense after all," admitted Carl. He rescued the chimney pot and carefully glued it back on to the roof.

"Now let's put this brilliant model on a high shelf so nothing else can happen before tomorrow," said Mum.

"And I'll start making a real hat for Jaye's doll," said Carl.

Picture plan

Illustration © 2010, Anna Godwin/Beehive Illustration.

Name _____ Date _____

Character storyline

What _____ does

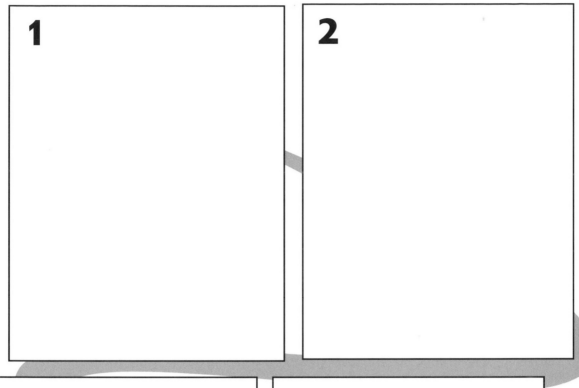

| 1 | 2 |
| 3 | 4 |

Red
Amber
Green

I can show a character's storyline in pictures. ☐

NARRATIVE
UNIT 2 Traditional stories

Literacy objectives

Speak and listen for a wide range of purposes in different contexts

Strand 1 Speaking
- Tell real and imagined stories using the conventions of familiar story language.

Strand 2 Listening and responding
- Respond to presentations by describing characters, repeating some highlights and commenting constructively.

Strand 4 Drama
- Present part of traditional stories, their own stories or work drawn from different parts of the curriculum for members of their own class.

Read and write for a range of purposes on paper and on screen

Strand 5 Word recognition: decoding (reading) and encoding (spelling)
- Read independently and with increasing fluency longer and less familiar texts.
- Know how to tackle unfamiliar words that are not completely decodable.
- Read high and medium frequency words independently and automatically.

Strand 6 Word structure and spelling
- Spell with increasing accuracy and confidence, drawing on word recognition and knowledge of word structure, and spelling patterns including common inflections and use of double letters.

Strand 7 Understanding and interpreting texts
- Draw together ideas and information from across a whole text, using simple signposts in the text.
- Give some reasons why things happen or characters change.

Strand 9 Creating and shaping texts
- Draw on knowledge and experience of texts in deciding and planning what and how to write.
- Select from different presentational features to suit particular writing purposes on paper and on screen.

Strand 11 Sentence structure and punctuation
- Write simple and compound sentences and begin to use subordination in relation to time and reason.

Key aspects of learning

Problem solving
- Children will respond to a task using trial and error and consider a range of possible solutions.

Creative thinking
- Children will generate imaginative ideas to make connections and see relationships between different modes of communication. Children will experiment with different modes of communication to respond to different points of view.

Communication
- Children will recognise communication in different modes. They will work collaboratively to discuss, plan and create a traditional tale.

Assessment focuses

Reading
AF2 *(understand, describe, select or retrieve information, events or ideas from texts and use quotation and reference to text).*
AF3 *(deduce, infer or interpret information, events or ideas from texts).*
AF4 *(identify and comment on the structure and organisation of texts, including grammatical and presentational features at text level).*
AF5 *(explain and comment on writers' use of language, including grammatical and literary features at word and sentence level).*

Writing
AF1 *(write imaginative, interesting and thoughtful texts).*
AF7 *(select appropriate and effective vocabulary).*

Speaking and listening
Speaking (speak with clarity, intonation and pace).
Listening and responding (listen to presentations, repeating some highlights and commenting constructively).
Drama (improvise and sustain roles).

Resources

Phase 1 activities
Photocopiable page, 'Hansel and Gretel (a)'
Photocopiable page, 'Good character or villain?' (versions 1 and 2)
Photocopiable page, 'Hansel and Gretel (b)'
Interactive activity, 'Who says what?'
Phase 2 activities
Photocopiable page, ' Hansel and Gretel (a)'
Photocopiable page, 'How will they look? What will they say?'
Photocopiable page, 'Hansel and Gretel storyboard'
Phase 3 activities
Photocopiable page, 'The Mystery Shoe'
Slideshow, 'The Mystery Shoe'
Photocopiable page, 'The Mystery Shoe on screen'
Periodic assessment
Photocopiable page, 'Narrative 2 Reading assessment text'
Interactive activity, 'Narrative 2 Reading assessment'
Photocopiable page, 'Narrative 2 Writing assessment'

Unit 2 ◻ Traditional stories

Learning outcomes	Assessment opportunity and evidence	Assessment focuses (AFs)	Success criteria
		Level 1	

Phase ① activities pages 29–30

Identifying different characters Children can express ideas about a character using evidence from the text to justify their opinion.	● Group activity where children listen to a reading of 'Hansel and Gretel (a)', identify opposing characters and play a simple listening game before completing the photocopiable page. ● Children's discussions, responses to the listening game and written responses on the photocopiable.	**Reading AF3** ● Reasonable inference at a basic level. ● Comments/questions about meaning of parts of text.	● I can describe a character from a story. ● I can read a traditional story and spot the 'good' and 'bad' characters.
Story dialogue Children can recognise and add dialogue to a story.	● Paired activity where children match dialogue to the relevant characters. ● Children's discussions and completion of the interactive activity.	**Reading AF2** ● Some simple points from familiar texts recalled. ● Some pages/sections of interest located.	I can find dialogue in a story.
Connectives Children understand that connectives can be used to link ideas and create tension in narrative.	● Group activity, where children listen to a rereading of 'Hansel and Gretel (a)', identify and highlight the time connectives and discuss the chosen words. ● Children's discussions and comments on the chosen words.	**Reading AF5** Comments on obvious features of language.	I can find time connectives in a story.

Phase ② activities pages 31–32

| **Reversing roles** Children can reverse the characteristics of characters in a traditional story. | ● Paired activity where children perform a role play, reversing the 'good' and 'bad' characters. ● Children's role plays, drawings and written responses on the photocopiable. | **Writing AF7** ● Mostly simple vocabulary. ● Communicates meaning through repetition of key words. | ● I can swap the roles of 'good' and 'bad' characters. ● I can write dialogue to match my new characters. |
| **Changing actions** Children can understand that text must match character action. | ● Group activity where children create a picture storyboard to match their written dialogue from the previous activity. ● Children's discussions and voting, pictorial storyboards and written notes. | **Reading AF3** ● Reasonable inference at a basic level. ● Comments/questions about meaning of parts of text. | ● I can understand that text must match what a character is like. ● I can draw a storyboard to match my new characters. |

Unit 2 ⬜ Traditional stories

Learning outcomes	Assessment opportunity and evidence	Assessment focuses (AFs)	Success criteria
		Level 1	
Phase ③ activities pages 32-33			
Reading a multimodal text Children understand that words, images and sounds can convey different elements of a narrative for a reader.	• Group activity where children compare a text version of a story with an interactive version. • Children's discussions and exploration of the interactive activity.	**Reading AF4** Some awareness of meaning of simple text features.	I can understand how a multimodal text uses sounds and images to tell a story.
Creating a multimodal text Children can write a traditional narrative using words, sounds and images to convey information about the main characters.	• Group activity where children write a new story featuring the characters from 'Cinderella and the Stepsister' and plan a multimodal version of their story. • Children's discussions, story plans and multimodal screen designs.	**Writing AF1** • Basic information and ideas conveyed through appropriate word choice. • Some descriptive language.	I can use sound, text and images to describe characters in a story.

Learning outcomes	Assessment opportunity and evidence	Assessment focuses (AFs)		Success criteria
		Level 2	Level 3	
Phase ① activities pages 29-30				
Identifying different characters Children can express ideas about a character using evidence from the text to justify their opinion.	• Group activity where children listen to a reading of 'Hansel and Gretel (a)', identify opposing characters and play a simple listening game before completing the photocopiable page. • Children's discussions, responses to the listening game and written responses on the photocopiable.	**Reading AF3** • Simple, plausible inference about events and information, using evidence from text. • Comments based on textual cues, sometimes misunderstood.	**Reading AF3** • Straightforward inference based on a single point of reference in the text. • Responses to text show meaning established at a literal level or based on personal speculation.	• I can describe a character from a story. • I can read a traditional story and spot the 'good' and 'bad' characters.
Story dialogue Children can recognise and add dialogue to a story.	• Paired activity where children match dialogue to the relevant character. • Children's discussions and completion of the interactive activity.	**Reading AF2** • Some specific straightforward information recalled. • Generally clear idea of where to look for information.	**Reading AF2** • Simple, most obvious points identified though there may also be some misunderstanding. • Some comments include quotations from or references to text, but not always relevant.	I can find dialogue in a story.

Unit 2 ▢ Traditional stories

Learning outcomes	Assessment opportunity and evidence	Assessment focuses (AFs)		Success criteria
		Level 2	**Level 3**	
Connectives Children understand that connectives can be used to link ideas and create tension in narrative.	● Group activity, where children listen to a rereading of 'Hansel and Gretel (a)', identify and highlight the time connectives and discuss the chosen words. ● Children's discussions and comments on the chosen words.	**Reading AF5** ● Some effective language choices noted. ● Some familiar patterns of language identified.	**Reading AF5** A few basic features of writer's language identified, but with little or no comment.	I can find time connectives in a story.

Phase ② activities pages 31–32

Learning outcomes	Assessment opportunity and evidence	Level 2	Level 3	Success criteria
Reversing roles Children can reverse the characteristics of characters in a traditional story.	● Paired activity where children perform a role play, reversing the 'good' and 'bad' characters. ● Children's role plays, drawings and written responses on the photocopiable.	**Writing AF7** ● Simple, often speech-like vocabulary conveys relevant meanings. ● Some adventurous word choices.	**Writing AF7** ● Simple, generally appropriate vocabulary used, limited in range. ● Some words selected for effect or occasion.	● I can swap the roles of 'good' and 'bad' characters. ● I can write dialogue to match my new characters.
Changing actions Children can understand that text must match character action.	● Group activity where children create a picture storyboard to match their written dialogue from the previous activity. ● Children's discussions and voting, pictorial storyboards and written notes.	**Reading AF3** ● Simple, plausible inference about events and information, using evidence from text. ● Comments based on textual cues, sometimes misunderstood.	**Reading AF3** ● Straightforward inference based on a single point of reference in the text. ● Responses to text show meaning established at a literal level or based on personal speculation.	● I can understand that text must match what a character is like. ● I can draw a storyboard to match my new characters.

Phase ③ activities pages 32–33

Learning outcomes	Assessment opportunity and evidence	Level 2	Level 3	Success criteria
Reading a multimodal text Children understand that words, images and sounds can convey different elements of a narrative for a reader.	● Group activity where children compare a text version of a story with an interactive version. ● Children's discussions and exploration of the interactive activity.	**Reading AF4** Some awareness of use of features of organisation.	**Reading AF4** A few basic features of organisation at text level identified, with little or no linked comment.	I can understand how a multimodal text uses sounds and images to tell a story.
Creating a multimodal text Children can write a traditional narrative using words, sounds and images to convey information about the main characters.	● Group activity where children write a new story featuring the characters from 'Cinderella and the Stepsister' and plan a multimodal version of their story. ● Children's discussions, story plans and multimodal screen designs.	**Writing AF1** ● Mostly relevant ideas and content, sometimes repetitive or sparse. ● Some apt word choices create interest. ● Brief comments, questions about events or actions suggest viewpoint.	**Writing AF1** ● Some appropriate ideas and content included. ● Some attempt to elaborate on basic information or events. ● Attempt to adopt viewpoint, though often not maintained or inconsistent.	I can use sound, text and images to describe characters in a story.

Phase ① Identifying different characters

Learning outcome
Children can express ideas about a character using evidence from the text to justify their opinion.

Success criteria
● I can describe a character from a story.
● I can read a traditional story and spot the 'good' and 'bad' characters.

Setting the context
Familiarise the children with some traditional stories, such as 'Cinderella' or 'Red Riding Hood'. Ensure that they are aware that these stories always have a 'good' character and a villain, and have used these terms when exploring the texts.

Assessment opportunity
Divide the class into groups of comparable ability. Give the children individual copies of the photocopiable page 'Hansel and Gretel (a)'. Read the story with each group. Ask the children to identify the female characters and discuss them. Then, give each child a piece of paper – with the word 'good' on one side, and the word 'villain' on the other. Play a game in which you say *I am...* Finish the sentence with either *Gretel* or *the Stepmother*, inviting the children to hold up the appropriate side of their paper. Do this a few times and observe who is unsure of the character distinction. Afterwards, hand out individual copies of the photocopiable page 'Good character or villain?' (version 1 or 2) for the children to complete.

Assessment evidence
At level 1, the children will recognise the difference between good and bad characters and they will make basic inferences using the story. At levels 2-3, the children's inferences about the characters may be based on one reference from the story. This activity will provide evidence towards Reading AF3.

Next steps
Support: If the children struggle with writing their answers, make some of the assessment oral and record accordingly.
Extension: Suggest the children write an additional section to the story, with Gretel and the Stepmother performing other actions to suit their characters.

Key aspects of learning
Creative thinking: Children will generate imaginative ideas to make connections and see relationships between different modes of communication. Children will experiment with different modes of communication to respond to different points of view.

Phase ① Story dialogue

Learning outcome
Children can recognise and add dialogue to a story.

Success criteria
I can find dialogue in a story.

Setting the context
The children should know the word 'dialogue' and have heard and seen it used in a story. Recap the story of Hansel and Gretel, and remind the children about the opposing characters (see previous activity).

Assessment opportunity
Put the children into pairs and give them the photocopiable page 'Hansel and Gretel (b)' to read. Remind them to check and re-read this text as they complete the first screen of the interactive activity 'Who says what?'. Afterwards, ask them if they think they could have placed the dialogue without referring to the text. Can they

guess what someone would say just by their personality and actions? Introduce the children to the second screen of the interactive activity and ask them to match the speech to the characters. Explain that this new dialogue doesn't appear in the story, but we should be able to make a good guess as to who would say what.

Assessment evidence
At level 1, the children will be able to place the dialogue on the first screen of the interactive activity but will need more discussion and some trial and error for the second screen. At levels 2–3, dialogue work should still provoke discussion but there should be greater awareness that a character's speech gives information about personality. The first screen of the interactive activity will provide evidence towards Reading AF2.

Next steps
Support: If the children struggle with the first screen suggest they work on one character at a time, finding what they say in the text and then searching for some of it on the screen.
Extension: Challenge the children to write their own dialogue for the characters in the story.

Key aspects of learning
Problem solving: Children will respond to a task using trial and error and consider a range of possible solutions.

Phase ① Connectives

Learning outcome
Children understand that connectives can be used to link ideas and create tension in narrative.

Success criteria
I can find time connectives in a story.

Setting the context
The children should have completed some preliminary work on the use of time connectives in a story. Display the photocopiable page 'Hansel and Gretel (a)' and re-read the story to the whole class. Select children to identify and highlight the time connectives in the text. Hold a discussion about the chosen words. Ask the children to suggest why they think the writer has used them?

Assessment evidence
At level 1, the children will notice some of the connectives but they are likely to need some support to achieve this. At levels 2–3, the children will identify most of the connectives in the story but their comments on the author's choice of connectives will be limited. This activity will provide evidence towards Reading AF5.

Next steps
Support: Create a list of time connectives for the children to identify in the text.
Extension: Suggest the children look at a recent story and challenge them to improve one page by adding some connectives.

Key aspects of learning
Communication: Children will recognise communication in different modes. They will work collaboratively to discuss, plan and create a traditional tale.

Learning outcome
Children can reverse the characteristics of characters in a traditional story.

Success criteria
- I can swap the roles of 'good' and 'bad' characters.
- I can write dialogue to match my new characters.

Setting the context
The children should have completed the previous two activities and have experience of role play. Re-read the story 'Hansel and Gretel (a)' from the photocopiable page. Remind the children of their previous work on character and dialogue, and recap the distinction between the 'good' character in the story and the villain.

Assessment opportunity
Put the children into pairs - one child to role-play Gretel and the other to take on the role of the Stepmother. Ask the children to use their face and body language to pose as their character in the first scene of the story, when the Stepmother is eating. Now suggest that the characters swap round: the Stepmother is the 'good' character and Gretel is now the villain. Let the children change their face and body language to match the character. (You might want to give each child a hat to wear, labelled 'S' or 'G', so that you can see whether children are performing their roles correctly.) Next, ask partners to improvise a conversation between the two characters in their changed roles. Once they have had time to explore and practise their roles, provide children with the photocopiable page 'How will they look? What will they say?' to complete the first half of the worksheet. Repeat the role-play activity so that children can then explore what the characters might say while in the forest and then ask them to complete the remainder of the worksheet.

Assessment evidence
At level 1, the children will understand character distinctions but may need reminders to stay in their altered role. At levels 2-3, the children will find the reversal easier and will improvise conversation readily. This activity will provide evidence towards Writing AF7.

Next steps
Support: Encourage partner role play as preparation for the written work. If necessary, use the role play to make your assessment.
Extension: Ask the children to observe a partner's pose and listen to their speech, to evaluate afterwards how realistic they were and how well their words matched their body language.

Key aspects of learning
Creative thinking: Children will generate imaginative ideas to make connections and see relationships between different modes of communication. Children will experiment with different modes of communication to respond to different points of view.

Learning outcome
Children can understand that text must match character action.

Success criteria
- I can understand that text must match what a character is like.
- I can draw a storyboard to match my new characters.

Setting the context
The children should have completed the previous activity 'Reversing roles'. Display the illustrations from the photocopiable page 'Hansel and Gretel storyboard'. Explain that they are part of the writer's planning storyboard for Hansel and Gretel. Give

the children their completed photocopiable pages from the previous activity. Ask individual children to read out their dialogue for the changed Gretel. Do the same for the changed Stepmother.

Assessment opportunity

Assess children's awareness of the incompatibility between the new characters' dialogue and their actions in the pictures. Ask them to hold up (or write and display on their whiteboards) a simple 'yes' or 'no' when you ask: *Do those words suit what the character is doing in the picture?* Give each child a sheet of paper with four numbered boxes on it. Invite them to use the boxes to create a new storyboard to match the dialogue on their photocopiable page. Ensure the children realise that the Stepmother must now do things that suit a 'good' character and Gretel now behaves as the 'bad' character.

Assessment evidence

At level 1, the children's storyboard will have less detail than at levels 2–3, and they may sometimes forget and let a character slip back into their former role. At levels 2–3, the children should be able to sustain the role reversal and their storyboards will show their ability to infer how characters will behave, using evidence from the dialogue. This activity will provide evidence towards Reading AF3.

Next steps

Support: Give the children a smaller storyboard, featuring just two squares, and suggest which events in the story they could change.
Extension: Suggest the children show their picture storyboard to a partner, using it as a prompt for oral storytelling.

Key aspects of learning

Creative thinking: Children will generate imaginative ideas to make connections and see relationships between different modes of communication. Children will experiment with different modes of communication to respond to different points of view.

Phase ③ Reading a multimodal text

Learning outcome
Children understand that words, images and sounds can convey different elements of a narrative for a reader.

Success criteria
I can understand how a multimodal text uses sounds and images to tell a story.

Setting the context
Ensure the children have used and discussed multimodal stories. Remind them of the opposing characters in a traditional story – the 'good' character and the villain. Display and read the photocopiable page 'The Mystery Shoe'. Afterwards, put the children into groups of comparable ability to re-read and discuss the short story, deciding who is the 'good' character and who is the villain.

Assessment opportunity
Ask the children if they enjoyed reading such a short story. Can they suggest ways to make it more interesting? Provide groups with a multimodal version of the story using the slideshow 'The Mystery Shoe'. Listen to their discussion to assess how the interactive activity adds to their understanding of the characters and enjoyment of the story. Encourage them to consider where sounds could be added to improve the slideshow. Make a list of their suggestions to revisit during the next activity. Ask the children to complete the photocopiable page 'The Mystery Shoe on screen'.

Assessment evidence
At level 1, the children will explain, in simple terms, what presentational features they liked in the slideshow. At levels 2–3, the children will have more sophisticated

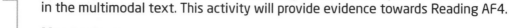

opinions about the impact made on them by the additional presentational features in the multimodal text. This activity will provide evidence towards Reading AF4.

Next steps
Support: Ask questions such as: *How did the screen image improve the story?*
Extension: Ask the children to consider their ideas for a better screen for the story and to draw it, marking where and what their hotspots would be. Simple drawing tools could be used to do the task on screen.

Key aspects of learning
Creative thinking: Children will generate imaginative ideas to make connections and see relationships between different modes of communication. Children will experiment with different modes of communication to respond to different points of view.
Communication: Children will recognise communication in different modes. They will work collaboratively to discuss, plan and create a traditional tale.

Phase ③ Creating a multimodal text

Learning outcome
Children can write a traditional narrative using words, sounds and images to convey information about the main characters.

Success criteria
I can use sound, text and images to describe characters in a story.

Setting the context
Ensure the children have used and discussed multimodal stories. Read aloud 'The Mystery Shoe', from the previous activity. Remind them of the multimodal version, display it and recap on the children's list of suggestions for new sounds.

Assessment opportunity
Put the children into small groups to use a computer to type another short story about Cinderella and her stepsister. Afterwards, ask them to draw on paper an accompanying screen, marking where and what hot spots or sounds they will provide to help the reader learn more about the two characters in their story.

Assessment evidence
At level 1, the children will need story suggestions. They should have ideas about two possible hot spots or sounds. At levels 2–3, the children will write more imaginative hot spots that add impact to the story. This activity will provide evidence towards Writing AF1.

Next steps
Support: Provide some possible scenarios for their stories, for example, the Stepsister has lost something; Cinderella is ill; the Stepsister wants more cake.
Extension: Have groups create their own interactive story using ICT.

Key aspects of learning
Creative thinking: Children will generate imaginative ideas to make connections and see relationships between different modes of communication. Children will experiment with different modes of communication to respond to different points of view.
Communication: Children will recognise communication in different modes. They will work collaboratively to discuss, plan and create a traditional tale.

NARRATIVE

NARRATIVE

Periodic assessment

Reading

Learning outcomes
- Children can express ideas about a character using evidence from the text.
- Children understand that connectives can be used to link ideas and create tension in narrative.

Success criteria
- I can describe characters from a story.
- I can understand that text must match what a character is like.
- I can find connectives in a story.

Setting the context
Children should have read some examples of traditional stories, and identified the 'good' and the 'bad' character (villain) in each. Recap on the original story of Hansel and Gretel referring to the text if necessary. Remind the children of the work they did in the previous activities, exploring the characters of Gretel and the Stepmother. Now, reveal to the children that you have a new version of the story to share. Read 'The true story of Hansel and Gretel' on the photocopiable page 'Narrative 2 Reading assessment text'.

Assessment opportunity
Let partners discuss the two important characters - Gretel and the Stepmother. Assess individual understanding of the characters and the relevance of dialogue and actions by using the interactive activity, 'Narrative 2 Reading assessment'. Ask the children to print their work once they have finished the activity. You could also use this opportunity to assess some children's ability to read aloud the story on the photocopiable page (up to level 3). As they are reading, ask them to pause to find a connective word in the text and discuss why the author may have used it.

Assessment evidence
At level 1, the children will need support in reading the text from the photocopiable page and the interactive activity screen. They are unlikely to be sure of connectives and may struggle with the concept of 'likely behaviour'. At levels 2-3, the children will usually read with fluency and independence and they should be able to point out and make basic comments on the use of some connective words in the text. They will also be able to understand and complete the interactive activity. This activity will help you judge the children's overall understanding of work in this unit and will provide evidence against Reading AF1, AF2 and AF5.

SCHOLASTIC

Periodic assessment

Writing

Learning outcomes
● Children can understand that text must match character action.
● Children can identify and add connectives.

Success criteria
● I can swap the roles of 'good' and 'bad' characters.
● I can write dialogue to match my new characters.
● I can identify and add connectives.

Setting the context
Ensure the children have read the two extracts of the story of 'Hansel and Gretel' used in Phase 1 (see page 29). They should have their pictorial storyboard and written character dialogue from the previous Phase 2 activities. Perform this assessment after the children have also read and explored 'The true story of Hansel and Gretel' in the Periodic reading activity for Unit 2.

Assessment opportunity
Re-read, 'Hansel and Gretel (b)' from the Phase 1 activity 'Story dialogue' (see page 29) and remind the children of their work on reversing roles. Ask them to look at the dialogue they created for a 'bad' Gretel and a 'good' Stepmother. Let them discuss their pictorial storyboards with a partner to remind themselves of the character actions that they devised to suit their new dialogue. Re-read 'The true story of Hansel and Gretel' and point out the linking time connectives. For example, *later, meanwhile, finally* and *then*. Ask the children to write their own story, again calling it 'The true story of Hansel and Gretel' but with text and dialogue to match their picture storyboard. Encourage children working at levels 2–3 to include some connectives. Afterwards, give everyone the photocopiable page 'Narrative 2 Writing assessment' to self-assess their story using the 'three stars and a wish' method.

Assessment evidence
At level 1, the children's stories are likely to be short and the children may need to be reminded to match them to their storyboard and dialogue. At levels 2–3, the children will enjoy writing longer stories, may add to their planned storyboard events, and use additional dialogue. They may need to be encouraged to re-read their finished story to look for places where connectives would improve the time sequence of the story. This activity will help you judge the children's overall understanding of work in this unit and provide evidence against Writing AF3, AF4 and AF7.

Name _____ Date _____

Good character or villain? (1)

Gretel	**Stepmother**

Which of these words tell you about Gretel?	Which of these words tell you about the Stepmother?

| greedy   cross   garden   brave | kind   happy   cruel   forest |

Does Gretel do good or bad things in this story?

_____

Does the Stepmother do good or bad things in this story?

_____

What does Gretel do?

_____

_____

_____

What does the Stepmother do?

_____

_____

_____

Red · Amber · Green — I can describe a character from a story. ☐

I can read a traditional story and spot the 'good' and 'bad' characters. ☐

Name   Date

How will they look?
What will they say?

◼ Draw how the changed characters will look.

◼ Write what they say in the speech bubbles.

Scene one: In the kitchen

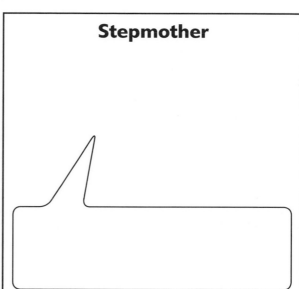

Scene two: In the forest

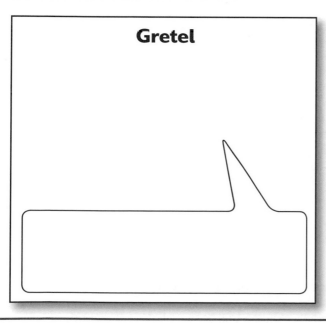

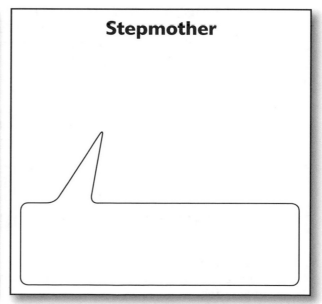

Red

Amber

Green

I can swap the roles of 'good' and 'bad' characters. ☐

I can write dialogue to match my new characters. ☐

NARRATIVE

UNIT 3 Different stories by the same author

Literacy objectives

Speak and listen for a wide range of purposes in different contexts

Strand 2 Listening and responding
- Listen to others in class, ask relevant questions and follow instructions.

Strand 3 Group discussion and interaction
- Work effectively in groups by ensuring that each group member takes a turn challenging, supporting and moving on.

Strand 4 Drama
- Adopt appropriate roles in small or large groups and consider alternative courses of action.

Read and write for a range of purposes on paper and on screen

Strand 5 Word recognition: decoding (reading) and encoding (spelling)
- Read independently and with increasing fluency longer and less familiar texts.
- Spell with increasing accuracy and confidence, drawing on word recognition and knowledge of word structure, and spelling patterns.
- Read high and medium frequency words independently and automatically.

Strand 6 Word structure and spelling
- Spell with increasing accuracy and confidence, drawing on word recognition and knowledge of word structure, and spelling patterns including common inflections and use of double letters.
- Read and spell less common alternative graphemes including trigraphs.

Strand 8 Engaging with and responding to texts
- Engage with books through exploring and enacting interpretations.
- Explain their reactions to texts, commenting on important aspects.

Strand 9 Creating and shaping texts
- Sustain form in narrative, including use of person and time.

Strand 10 Text structure and organisation
- Use planning to establish clear sections for writing.

Strand 11 Sentence structure and punctuation
- Compose sentences using tense consistently (present and past).

Key aspects of learning

Reasoning
- Children will compare texts and give evidence for the opinions they form.

Evaluation
- As they learn about features of an author's style, children will become better equipped to make judgements about the type of books they enjoy reading.

Social skills
- Children participate in a collaborative group activity. They will learn about taking turns, listening to others and reaching agreement.

Key aspects of learning (continued)

Communication
- Children will develop their ability to discuss as they work collaboratively in paired, group and whole-class contexts. They will communicate outcomes orally, in writing and through ICT if appropriate.

Assessment focuses

Reading
AF3 *(deduce, infer or interpret information, events or ideas from texts).*
AF5 *(explain and comment on writers' use of language, including grammatical and literary features at word and sentence level).*
AF6 *(identify and comment on writers' purposes and viewpoints, and the overall effect of the text on the reader).*

Writing
AF1 *(write imaginative, interesting and thoughtful texts).*
AF3 *(organise and present whole texts effectively, sequencing and structuring information, ideas and events).*

Speaking and listening
Listening and responding (listen to presentations, repeating some highlights and commenting constructively).
Group discussion and interaction (take turns).
Drama (improvise and sustain roles).

Resources

Phase 1 activities
Photocopiable page, 'Aristotle (a)'
Photocopiable page, 'Reading a story' (versions 1 and 2)
Photocopiable page, 'The Golden Goose'
Photocopiable page, 'Stories by the same author' (versions 1 and 2)
Phase 2 activities
Photocopiable page, 'Aristotle (a)'
Photocopiable page, 'Asking Aristotle'
Photocopiable page, 'The Golden Goose'
Interactive activity, 'Finding out about Farmer Skint'
Phase 3 activities
Photocopiable page, 'Book evaluation'
Phase 4 activities
Photocopiable page, 'Aristotle (a)'
Photocopiable page, 'My story idea'
Periodic assessment
Photocopiable page, 'Narrative 3 Reading assessment text'
Photocopiable page, 'Narrative 3 Reading assessment'

Unit 3 ▢ Different stories by the same author

Learning outcomes	Assessment opportunity and evidence	Assessment focuses (AFs)		Success criteria
		Level 1		
Phase ① activities pages 43-44				
Reacting to a story Children can talk about a text and explain their reaction to it.	● Paired activity where children respond to a text extract using facial expressions and body language. ● Facial expressions and partner discussions indicate text recognition. ● Children's completed photocopiables show understanding of the text.	**Reading AF6** Some simple comments about preferences, mostly linked to own experience.		I can describe how I feel about a story.
Reacting to an author Children can identify characteristics of the author's style.	● Paired activity where children compare two stories by the same author, using the Internet to learn more about the author and their works. ● Children's discussions and written answers on the differentiated photocopiable.	**Reading AF5** Comments on obvious features of language.		● I can describe how I feel about a story. ● I can describe an author's style.
Phase ② activities pages 44-45				
Investigating characters Children can investigate character by asking questions and answering them in role.	● Paired activity where children explore a character through role play and dialogue improvisation. ● Children's discussions, role plays of the characters and written responses on the photocopiable.	**Reading AF3** ● Reasonable inference at a basic level. ● Comments/questions about meaning of parts of text.		I can explore the thoughts and feelings of a story character.
Looking for evidence Children can make inferences about characters and use the text to support their answers.	● Paired activity where children role play detectives, searching a text for clues about a character. ● Children's discussions of the text and printed results from the interactive activity.	**Reading AF3** ● Reasonable inference at a basic level. ● Comments/questions about meaning of parts of text.		I can describe a character using the story to support my ideas.
Phase ③ activities pages 46-47				
Evaluating a whole story Children can sustain interest in and form an opinion of a whole story.	● Activity where children read and discuss a whole story before completing an evaluation. ● Independent reading. ● Children's written book evaluations.	**Reading AF6** Some simple comments about preferences, mostly linked to own experience.		I can read and evaluate a whole story.

Unit 3   Different stories by the same author

Learning outcomes	Assessment opportunity and evidence	Assessment focuses (AFs)	Success criteria
		Level 1	
Working in a group Children can work as a member of a group to discuss and reach agreement over a task.	• Paired or grouped activity where children compare and discuss their book evaluations from the previous activity and recommend and present a book to the class. • Children's discussions and oral presentations to the class.	**Reading AF6** Some simple comments about preferences, mostly linked to own experience.	I can work as part of a group.

Phase ④ activities pages 47–48

Building ideas Children can discuss ideas for a new story and its main characters.	• Paired and grouped activity where children choose an animal to write about, using known texts for inspiration. • Children's role play and improvised dialogue show evolving ideas. • Children's completed photocopiables.	**Writing AF1** • Basic information and ideas conveyed through appropriate word choice. • Some descriptive language.	I can use what I read to help me write.
Planning a story Children can plan a sustained story about a familiar character.	• Activity where children explore and develop their ideas from the previous activity using partner discussion and role play and then compile a structured pictorial plan with notes for their animal story. • Children's story plans.	**Writing AF3** • Some formulaic phrases indicate start/end of text. • Events/ideas sometimes in appropriate order.	I can use what I read to help me write.

Learning outcomes	Assessment opportunity and evidence	Assessment focuses (AFs)		Success criteria
		Level 2	**Level 3**	
Phase ① activities pages 43–44				
Reacting to a story Children can talk about a text and explain their reaction to it.	• Paired activity where children respond to a text extract using facial expressions and body language. • Facial expressions and partner discussions indicate text recognition. • Children's completed photocopiables show understanding of the text.	**Reading AF6** • Some awareness that writers have viewpoints and purposes. • Simple statements about likes and dislikes in reading, sometimes with reasons.	**Reading AF6** • Comments identify main purpose. • Express personal response but with little awareness of writer's viewpoint or effect on reader.	I can describe how I feel about a story.
Reacting to an author Children can identify characteristics of the author's style.	• Paired activity where children compare two stories by the same author, using the Internet to learn more about the author and their works. • Children's discussions and written answers on the photocopiable.	**Reading AF5** • Some effective language choices noted. • Some familiar patterns of language identified.	**Reading AF5** A few basic features of writer's language identified, but with little or no comment.	• I can describe how I feel about a story. • I can describe an author's style.

Unit 3 📖 Different stories by the same author

Learning outcomes	Assessment opportunity and evidence	Assessment focuses (AFs)		Success criteria
		Level 2	Level 3	
Phase ② activities pages 44–45				
Investigating characters Children can investigate character by asking questions and answering them in role.	● Paired activity where children explore a character through role play and dialogue improvisation. ● Children's discussions, role plays of the characters and written responses on the photocopiable.	**Reading AF3** ● Simple, plausible inference about events and information, using evidence from text. ● Comments based on textual cues, sometimes misunderstood.	**Reading AF3** ● Straightforward inference based on a single point of reference in the text. ● Responses to text show meaning established at a literal level or based on personal speculation.	I can explore the thoughts and feelings of a story character.
Looking for evidence Children can make inferences about characters and use the text to support their answers.	● Paired activity where children role play detectives, searching a text for clues about a character. ● Children's discussions of the text and printed results from the interactive activity.	**Reading AF3** ● Simple, plausible inference about events and information, using evidence from text. ● Comments based on textual cues, sometimes misunderstood.	**Reading AF3** ● Straightforward inference based on a single point of reference in the text. ● Responses to text show meaning established at a literal level or based on personal speculation.	I can describe a character using the story to support my ideas.
Phase ③ activities pages 46–47				
Evaluating a whole story Children can sustain interest in and form an opinion of a whole story.	● Activity where children read and discuss a whole story before completing an evaluation. ● Independent reading. ● Children's written book evaluations.	**Reading AF6** ● Some awareness that writers have viewpoints and purposes. ● Simple statements about likes and dislikes in reading, sometimes with reasons.	**Reading AF6** ● Comments identify main purpose. ● Express personal response but with little awareness of writer's viewpoint or effect on reader.	I can read and evaluate a whole story.
Working in a group Children can work as a member of a group to discuss and reach agreement over a task.	● Paired or grouped activity where children compare and discuss their book evaluations from the previous activity and recommend and present a book to the class. ● Children's discussions and oral presentation.	**Reading AF6** ● Some awareness that writers have viewpoints and purposes, *eg 'it tells you how to do.* ● Simple statements about likes and dislikes in reading, sometimes with reasons.	**Reading AF6** ● Comments identify main purpose. ● Express personal response but with little awareness of writer's viewpoint or effect on reader.	I can work as part of a group.
Phase ④ activities pages 47–48				
Building ideas Children can discuss ideas for a new story and its main characters.	● Paired and grouped activity where children choose an animal to write about, using known texts for inspiration. ● Children's role play and improvised dialogue. ● Children's completed photocopiables.	**Writing AF1** ● Mostly relevant ideas and content, sometimes repetitive or sparse. ● Some apt word choices create interest. ● Brief comments, questions about events or actions suggest viewpoint.	**Writing AF1** ● Some appropriate ideas and content included. ● Some attempt to elaborate on basic information or events. ● Attempt to adopt viewpoint, though often not maintained or inconsistent.	I can use what I read to help me write.
Planning a story Children can plan a sustained story about a familiar character.	● Activity where children explore and develop their ideas from the previous activity, using partner discussion and role play, and then write a structured plan for their animal story. ● Children's story plans.	**Writing AF3** ● Some basic sequencing of ideas or material. ● Openings and/or closings sometimes signalled.	**Writing AF3** ● Some attempt to organise ideas with related points placed next to each other. ● Openings and closings usually signalled. ● Some attempt to sequence ideas or material logically.	I can use what I read to help me write.

Phase ① Reacting to a story

Learning outcome
Children can talk about a text and explain their reaction to it.

Success criteria
I can describe how I feel about a story.

Setting the context
Prior to this assessment, ensure that the children have experience of expressing their own reactions to books and commenting on a writer's style and characteristics. They should also have written simple book reviews. Share the text extract, 'Aristotle (a)' on the photocopiable page. Ask the children to show their immediate reactions to the text using a facial expression.

Assessment opportunity
Invite the children to show their expression to a partner, and explain and justify their reaction. Give the children their own copies of the photocopiable page 'Aristotle (a)' to read and discuss together before giving everyone the photocopiable page 'Reading a story' (version 1 or 2) to complete.

Assessment evidence
At level 1, the children will probably express a reaction to just one part of the text, often the final part. At levels 2–3, the children will demonstrate greater awareness of different episodes within the story. Their written answers should, similarly, contain greater detail. This activity will provide evidence towards Reading AF6.

Next steps
Support: If the children struggle with reading the text independently, offer support by re-reading it with them. Suggest they give oral answers to a partner before they write them down.
Extension: Ask the children to read a similar-length extract from their current reading book. Give them another copy of version 2 of the photocopiable page 'Reading a story' to review it. Which writer gets the higher score out of 10?

Key aspects of learning
Evaluation: As they learn about features of an author's style, children will become better equipped to make judgements about the type of books they enjoy reading.
Communication: Children will develop their ability to discuss as they work collaboratively in paired, group and whole-class contexts. They will communicate outcomes orally, in writing and through ICT if appropriate.

Phase ① Reacting to an author

Learning outcome
Children can identify characteristics of the author's style.

Success criteria
● I can describe how I feel about a story.
● I can describe an author's style.

Setting the context
The children should have already completed the previous activity. Re-read the text 'Aristotle (a)'. Tell the children that they are going to read part of a different story by Dick King-Smith.

Assessment opportunity
Work with each group, so that you can easily recognise and record the children's level of comprehension. Give the children the photocopiable page 'The Golden Goose' and read it with them. Put the children into pairs to discuss if and how it is similar to the author's other story. Can they identify any simple characteristics

NARRATIVE

of the author's style? For example, the setting or the detailed descriptions of the different animals. Ask them to talk about how they could find out more about this author. Watch and listen for children who make little oral contribution. Give the children the photocopiable page 'Stories by the same author' (version 1 or 2) to complete. Provide access to the website www.channel4learning.com/sites/bookbox/authors/kingsmith/ to help children answer question four.

Assessment evidence
At level 1, the children will need more prompting during their discussion and may be less confident in their use of the website. At levels 2–3, the children will discuss more readily, have opinions about the writer's style and be able to justify their opinions with reference to the text. This activity will provide evidence towards Reading AF5.

Next steps
Support: If the children struggle with written answers, encourage oral answers first. Offer assistance in using the website.
Extension: Suggest the children do additional reading from the book, *The Golden Goose*, so that they can comment in more detail on the author's style.

Key aspects of learning
Reasoning: Children will compare texts and give evidence for the opinions they form.
Evaluation: As they learn about features of an author's style, children will become better equipped to make judgements about the type of books they enjoy reading.

Phase ② Investigating characters

Learning outcome
Children can investigate character by asking questions and answering them in role.

Success criteria
I can explore the thoughts and feelings of a story character.

Setting the context
Prior to this assessment, the children should understand that characters form a key element of a story. They should also be aware that not all characters have to be human. Give the children the photocopiable page 'Aristotle (a)' and read it with them. Ask the children who they think the main character is. Suggest that it would be interesting to know more about what Aristotle thinks and feels.

Assessment opportunity
Put the children into pairs - one partner to role play the cat, the other to act as an interviewer. The child playing the interviewer should ask their partner three questions. Afterwards, they can swap roles. Remind pairs to stay in role and to keep thinking back to the story and the character of Aristotle, to ensure their responses match with the text. Afterwards, give the children the photocopiable page 'Asking Aristotle' to complete. For the children working at level 1, ask them to explain the reasons for their answers. At levels 2–3, let the children colour-code their answer bubbles and then underline, in the matching colour, the part of the text that justifies each answer.

Assessment evidence
At level 1, the children will enjoy the role play, but may need prompting when they play the interviewer and may need to be reminded to relate the cat's thinking to what happens in the text. After completing the photocopiable page 'Asking Aristotle', they may be able to say which part of the story supports one of their answers. At levels 2–3, the children's oral questions will be more interesting and role play answers should demonstrate good understanding of the character in the text. In the colour-coding exercise, they should underline the relevant text for two of their answers. This activity will provide evidence towards Reading AF3.

▷ **Next steps**

Support: If children struggle with writing answers, suggest they explain them orally to you first.
Extension: Let the children devise a few more questions and answers for Aristotle.

Key aspects of learning
Reasoning: Children will compare texts and give evidence for the opinions they form.

Phase ② Looking for evidence

Learning outcome
Children can make inferences about characters and use the text to support their answers.

Success criteria
I can describe a character using the story to support my ideas.

Setting the context
The children will need to have completed the previous activity. Start by reminding them of the work they did, investigating the character of Aristotle. Hand out copies of the photocopiable page 'The Golden Goose' and re-read it together. Explain that they are going to become character detectives again – this time investigating the character of Farmer Skint.

Assessment opportunity
Put the children into pairs to re-read *The Golden Goose* text extract with their partner and discuss the clues that tell us about the type of person Farmer Skint is. Let them test their findings by doing the interactive activity 'Finding out about Farmer Skint'. Get them to print off their work once the activity has been completed.

Assessment evidence
At level 1, the children may need help reading the text but should identify Farmer Skint's interest, care and gentleness with animals. At levels 2–3, the children will use partnered discussion to search for character clues and should score adequately in the interactive activity. Some may forget to combine the interactive activity with checking the text. This activity will provide evidence towards Reading AF3.

Next steps
Support: If children struggle with the interactive activity, re-read the text to them and offer prompts to help draw out the answers.
Extension: Challenge the children to write a paragraph about Farmer Skint's character, making reference to supporting evidence from the text.

Key aspects of learning
Communication: Children will develop their ability to discuss as they work collaboratively in paired, group and whole-class contexts. They will communicate outcomes orally, in writing and through ICT if appropriate.

Phase ③ Evaluating a whole story

Learning outcome
Children can sustain interest in and form an opinion of a whole story.

Success criteria
I can read and evaluate a whole story.

Setting the context
Collect a number of short animal stories by Dick King-Smith. Ensure there is a copy of one complete story for each child.

Assessment opportunity
Make sure that a number (about four to six) of Dick King-Smith's stories are studied within the class. Allow time for each child to read one complete animal story by the author. If necessary, adapt the task to suit reading ability and time constraints. For example, the children could read sections of a story and then confer in pairs or groups to piece together the complete story, or an adult could read aloud/ paraphrase sections of the story. Each time a book is finished, give everyone the photocopiable page 'Book evaluation' to complete.

Assessment evidence
At level 1, the children will read and evaluate one of Dick King-Smith's picture stories and will benefit from adult support. At levels 2–3, the children will use a mixture of independent and collaborative reading, and will complete the photocopiable page 'Book evaluation' independently. This activity will provide evidence towards Reading AF6.

Next steps
Support: If children struggle with the reading task, reduce it to cover a small section of the story.
Extension: Suggest the children repeat the task with a second Dick King-Smith story.

Key aspects of learning
Evaluation: As they learn about features of an author's style, children will become better equipped to make judgements about the type of books they enjoy reading.

Phase ③ Working in a group

Learning outcome
Children can work as a member of a group to discuss and reach agreement over a task.

Success criteria
I can work as part of a group.

Setting the context
Revisit the books that were read as part of the previous activity. Return to each child their completed photocopiable page 'Book evaluation' (from the previous activity) and remind them of what they did.

Assessment opportunity
Put the children who read the same book into pairs or small groups, so that they can remind each other about the story and compare their evaluations. Afterwards, move the children into groups where each child has evaluated a different book. Ask the children to hold a group discussion, telling one another about their books. Can they identify common features? (Perhaps something funny always happened.) Each group must then decide which book to recommend to the rest of the class. Groups should share the task of reporting and justifying their recommendation. Is there a clear class favourite?

Assessment evidence
At level 1, the children will need help remembering their story and may focus only on parts of their book evaluation. Their group discussion contribution may be short but should be relevant. At levels 2–3, the children will remember their story more readily, feel ownership of their evaluation, and should make an adequate contribution to the group task. This activity will provide evidence towards Reading AF6.

Next steps
Support: If the children struggle with remembering their story, use adult support to retell the story.
Extension: Suggest the children produce a written report on their group discussion and its outcome.

Key aspects of learning
Reasoning: Children will compare texts and give evidence for the opinions they form.
Social skills: Children participate in a collaborative group activity. They will learn about taking turns, listening to others and reaching agreement.
Communication: Children will develop their ability to discuss as they work collaboratively in paired, group and whole-class contexts. They will communicate outcomes orally, in writing and through ICT if appropriate.

Phase ④ Building ideas

Learning outcome
Children can discuss ideas for a new story and its main characters.

Success criteria
I can use what I read to help me write.

Setting the context
Ensure the children are familiar with the character of Aristotle from the photocopiable page 'Aristotle (a)'. Remind the children of the kitten's foolhardy ways, risk-taking and tendency to be involved in accidents.

Assessment opportunity
Do this assessment with a group of children so that you can note the extent of an individual's contribution. Explain that you want them to create a story about an animal. Give a minute's thinking time before the children hold up the name of their chosen animal on their individual whiteboard. Let the children talk to a partner about their ideas, discussing what their animal would be like, how it would behave, what sort of things would happen and so on. Encourage partners to try out their story ideas with improvised dialogue and role play, sometimes exploring alternative courses of action. Watch and listen as you assess the children's ability to use familiar characters as inspiration. Afterwards, give the children the photocopiable page 'My story idea' to self-assess their progress.

Assessment evidence
At level 1, the children will have basic story ideas, but will need prompting with suggestions and questions. At levels 2–3, the children's role play and written notes will be more imaginative and independent. This activity will provide evidence towards Writing AF1.

Next steps
Support: If children struggle with ideas for the content of a story, remind them of what Dick King-Smith's characters said and did, in particular, Aristotle.
Extension: Suggest children do a peer-assessment of their work partner, using the same format as the photocopiable page, 'My story idea', but changing 'I' and 'my' as required.

NARRATIVE

Key aspects of learning
Communication: Children will develop their ability to discuss as they work collaboratively in paired, group and whole-class contexts. They will communicate outcomes orally, in writing and through ICT if appropriate.

Phase ④ Planning a story

Learning outcome
Children can plan a sustained story about a familiar character.

Success criteria
I can use what I read to help me write.

Setting the context
Remind the children of their discussion and ideas from the previous activity. Return the children's completed photocopiable page 'My story idea' and then put them back into the same pairs to talk through their ideas – adding new ones if they wish.

Assessment opportunity
As the children discuss their ideas, suggest that they add notes to their photocopiable page 'My story idea', as their stories and characters evolve. Next, give children a sheet of paper with the section headings: 'opening', 'something happens', 'events to sort it out' and 'ending'. Under each heading, invite the children to write notes for their final plan. At level 1, encourage the children to draw a picture for each section instead and write only brief notes.

Assessment evidence
At level 1, the children's plans will be mainly pictorial. At levels 2–3, the children's plans should be written notes that form a clear guide for a future, written story. This activity will provide evidence towards Writing AF3.

Next steps
Support: If children struggle with written notes, concentrate on producing a pictorial plan instead.
Extension: Remind the children about the role of connectives in linking parts of a story. Suggest children make a note on their planning sheets of any connectives that they think they will find useful when they write the story.

Key aspects of learning
Communication: Children will develop their ability to discuss as they work collaboratively in paired, group and whole-class contexts. They will communicate outcomes orally, in writing and through ICT if appropriate.

Periodic assessment

Reading

Learning outcomes

- Children can talk about a text and explain their reaction to it.
- Children can make inferences about characters and use the text to support their answers.

Success criteria

- I can describe how I feel about a story.
- I can describe an author's style.
- I can describe a character using the story to support my ideas.

Setting the context

Give the children the experience of reading a complete story. Ensure they have read extracts from other books by the same author and have identified some characteristics of his or her writing. Display the photocopiable page 'Narrative 3 Reading assessment text' and provide the story context: *Aristotle, the cat, has wandered into a sleeping dog's kennel, and the dog has just woken up.* Read the text aloud and ask the children to show their reaction to the text using facial expressions. Ask them to explain and justify their reactions to a partner.

Assessment opportunity

Give the children a copy of the text to re-read in small groups. Assess individual understanding of the text and its characters using the photocopiable page 'Narrative 3 Reading assessment'. Children who are working at levels 2-3 will demonstrate a greater appreciation of the words used in the text.

Assessment evidence

At level 1, the children will understand what is happening in the pictures on the photocopiable page. They will identify a character and an emotion, but may fail to find textual evidence. At levels 2-3, the children will cope well with most of the questions although some of their answers may lack substance. This activity will help you judge the children's overall understanding of work in this unit and provide evidence against Reading AF2, AF3, AF5 and AF6.

NARRATIVE

Periodic assessment

Writing

Learning outcomes
● Children can plan and write a sustained story about a familiar character.
● Children can use the past tense, third person and can include some dialogue and detail to add interest.

Success criteria
● I can use what I read to help me write.
● I can use the past tense, third person and can include some dialogue and detail to add interest.

Setting the context
Ensure the children have completed the phase 4 activities. Display the extract 'Aristotle (b)' from the photocopiable page 'Narrative 3 Reading assessment text' or any Dick King-Smith extract that contains characters and dialogue. Remind the children about their story plans, and return their photocopiable pages, 'My story idea' and 'Story planner' (from Unit 1, Phase 3 'Story planning'). Talk about the text on display. Draw attention to the author's use of dialogue, the third person and the past tense.

Assessment opportunity
Ask the children to use their plans to write an animal story. Encourage them to include dialogue and to choose descriptive words carefully. Suggest they pause every so often to re-read what they have written and to check that they have used the third person and the past tense consistently.

Assessment evidence
At level 1, the children's stories may be short, the plot simple and the ending abrupt. They may slip between third- and first-person narrative and be erratic in their use of the past tense. At levels 2–3, the children should write a story with a clearer, four-stage structure and should be mainly consistent in their use of the third person and the past tense. This activity will help you judge the children's overall understanding of work in this unit and provide evidence against Writing AF1, AF2, AF3, AF7 and AF8.

The Golden Goose

Out of the darkness of the hut into the brightness of a lovely May morning they all came, and what he now saw made Farmer Skint catch his breath.

Four of the downy goslings were a pale yellowish colour, like most goslings are, but the fifth one was a wonderful bright gold, all over. Even its beak was gold, as were its little webbed feet.

Out of the golden egg, thought Farmer Skint dazedly, has come a golden gosling that will grow into a golden goose!

As the geese stood around him, waiting for the food in the bucket that the farmer was carrying, the golden gosling waddled right up to his feet and stood looking at him with eyes that were not only bright with intelligence but also golden in colour.

Something made poor unfortunate Farmer Skint squat down on his heels and put out a hand and stroke the gosling's golden back. Had he tried to do this to its brothers or sisters, they would surely have backed away, but the golden gosling stood quite still and even nodded its little head as though it was enjoying his touch.

NARRATIVE

| Name | Date |

Asking Aristotle

- ◼ Read the story of *Aristotle* again.
- ◼ Imagine that he is being asked these questions.
- ◼ Write what you think he would say.

Are you interested in finding out about places?

Have you got a good sense of smell?

What food do you enjoy?

Are you a bit greedy?

Red
Amber
Green

I can explore the thoughts and feelings of a story character. ☐

Name   Date

My story idea

The animal's name will be:

The title of my story will be:

I discussed my story idea with:

I am _____ with my story idea.

(pleased, disappointed)

This is because:

My story idea is about this animal:

The animal looks like this:

I can use what I read to help me write. 🔲

Red

Amber

Green

NARRATIVE

UNIT 4 Extended stories/ Significant authors

Literacy objectives

Speak and listen for a wide range of purposes in different contexts

Strand 2 Listening and responding
- Respond to presentations by describing characters, repeating some highlights and commenting constructively.

Strand 4 Drama
- Present part of traditional stories, their own stories or work drawn from different parts of the curriculum for members of their own class.

Read and write for a range of purposes on paper and on screen

Strand 5 Word recognition: decoding (reading) and encoding (spelling)
- Read independently and with increasing fluency longer and less familiar texts.
- Spell with increasing accuracy and confidence, drawing on word recognition and knowledge of word structure, and spelling patterns.
- Know how to tackle unfamiliar words that are not completely decodable.
- Read and spell less common alternative graphemes including trigraphs.
- Read high and medium frequency words independently and automatically.

Strand 6 Word structure and spelling
- Spell with increasing accuracy and confidence, drawing on word recognition and knowledge of word structure, and spelling patterns including common inflections and use of double letters.
- Read and spell less common alternative graphemes including trigraphs.

Strand 7 Understanding and interpreting texts
- Give some reasons why things happen or characters change.

Strand 8 Engaging with and responding to texts
- Engage with books through exploring and enacting interpretations.

Strand 9 Creating and shaping texts
- Sustain form in narrative, including use of person and time.

Strand 10 Text structure and organisation
- Use appropriate language to make sections hang together.

Key aspects of learning

Evaluation
- Children will discuss success criteria for their written work, give feedback to others and judge the quality of their own writing.

Self-awareness
- As they work on an extended piece of writing, children will learn how to organise their own work and how to maintain their concentration to complete a polished story.

Communication
- Children will develop their ability to discuss as they work collaboratively in paired, group and whole-class contexts. They will communicate outcomes orally, in writing and through ICT if appropriate.

Assessment focuses

Reading

AF2 *(understand, describe, select or retrieve information, events or ideas from texts and use quotation and reference to text).*
AF3 *(deduce, infer or interpret information, events or ideas from texts).*
AF6 *(identify and comment on writers' purposes and viewpoints and the overall effect of the text on the reader).*

Writing

AF1 *(write imaginative, interesting and thoughtful texts).*
AF3 *(organise and present whole texts effectively, sequencing and structuring information, ideas and events).*
AF7 *(select appropriate and effective vocabulary).*

Speaking and listening

Listening and responding (listen to presentations, repeating some highlights and commenting constructively).
Drama (work with others in a performance; evaluate performances).

Resources

Phase 1 activities
Photocopiable page, 'The Worst Witch Saves the Day' (extract 1)
Interactive activity, 'Answering wh- questions'
Photocopiable page, 'The Worst Witch Saves the Day' (extract 2)
Photocopiable page, 'Extending the story'
Phase 2 activities
Interactive activity, 'Follow the sequence'
Photocopiable page, 'The Worst Witch Saves the Day' (extract 2)
Photocopiable page, 'The Worst Witch Saves the Day' (extract 3)
Photocopiable page, 'Finding links'
Photocopiable page, 'Picture prompts'
Phase 3 activities
Photocopiable page, 'The Worst Witch Saves the Day' (extract 1)
Photocopiable page, 'Working together on a drama'
Photocopiable page, 'Theatre critic'

Unit 4 ▨ Extended stories/Significant authors

Learning outcomes	Assessment opportunity and evidence	Assessment focuses (AFs)	Success criteria
		Level 1	
Phase ① activities pages 59-60			
Understanding the story opening Children can make predictions about a text and discuss the way characters develop across a story.	● Paired activity where children identify characteristics of a story opening and explore a character's thoughts. ● Children's discussions, role play and written comments.	**Reading AF2** ● Some simple points from familiar texts recalled. ● Some pages/sections of interest located. **Writing AF7** ● Mostly simple vocabulary. ● Communicates meaning through repetition of key words.	● I can describe what might happen next in a story. ● I can describe how characters change in a story.
Making predictions Children can make predictions about a text and discuss the way characters develop across a story.	● Paired activity where children compare two story extracts and discuss how characters and events have changed and record their ideas for possible future events in the story. ● Children's role play and discussion, written comments and completed photocopiable.	**Reading AF3** ● Reasonable inference at a basic level. ● Comments/questions about meaning of parts of text.	● I can describe what might happen next in a story. ● I can describe how characters change in a story.
Phase ② activities pages 61-62			
Following a sequence Children can understand that a story has a logical sequence of events.	● Paired activity where children complete an interactive sequencing activity, compare two text extracts and record plot and character links. ● Children's discussions and written responses on the completed photocopiable.	**Reading AF2** ● Some simple points from familiar texts recalled. ● Some pages/sections of interest located.	I can identify events in a story.
Making a storyboard Children can plan a story that has a logical sequence of events.	● Paired activity where children plan their own story. ● Children's discussions and their pictorial storyboards.	**Writing AF3** ● Some formulaic phrases indicate start/end of text. ● Events/ideas sometimes in appropriate order.	● I can plan and write a complete story. ● I can plan a story that has a sequence of events.
Phase ③ activities pages 62-63			
Working in a group Children can work as a member of a group to present a scene from a known story to an audience.	● Paired and group activity where children freeze-frame a key moment from a story and plan a dramatisation of it. ● Teacher observation and group interaction. ● Children's completed self-assessment of their group work.	**Reading AF6** Some simple comments about preferences, mostly linked to own experience.	I can work with a group to plan and present a drama.

Unit 4 ◾ Extended stories/Significant authors

Learning outcomes	Assessment opportunity and evidence	Assessment focuses (AFs) Level 1	Success criteria
Improving presentation Children can respond to presentations by making constructive comments.	● Group activity where children present their dramatisation to the class and the audience review the performances. ● Teacher observation and group performances. ● Children's completed performance reviews.	**Writing AF1** ● Basic information and ideas conveyed through appropriate word choice. ● Some descriptive language.	● I can work with a group to plan and present a drama. ● I can comment on the presentations of others.

Learning outcomes	Assessment opportunity and evidence	Assessment focuses (AFs)		Success criteria
		Level 2	**Level 3**	
Phase ① activities pages 59-60				
Understanding the story opening Children can make predictions about a text and discuss the way characters develop across a story.	● Paired activity where children identify characteristics of a story opening and explore a character's thoughts. ● Children's discussions, role play and written comments.	**Reading AF2** ● Some specific straightforward information recalled. ● Generally clear idea of where to look for information. **Writing AF7** ● Simple, often speech-like vocabulary conveys relevant meanings. ● Some adventurous word choices.	**Reading AF2** ● Simple, most obvious points identified though there may also be some misunderstanding. ● Some comments include quotations from or references to text, but not always relevant. **Writing AF7** ● Simple, generally appropriate vocabulary used, limited in range. ● Some words selected for effect or occasion.	● I can describe what might happen next in a story. ● I can describe how characters change in a story.
Making predictions Children can make predictions about a text and discuss the way characters develop across a story.	● Paired activity where children compare two story extracts and discuss how characters and events have changed and record their ideas for possible future events in the story. ● Children's role play and discussion, written comments and completed photocopiable.	**Reading AF3** ● Simple, plausible inference about events and information, using evidence from text. ● Comments based on textual cues, sometimes misunderstood.	**Reading AF3** ● Straightforward inference based on a single point of reference in the text. ● Responses to text show meaning established at a literal level, or based on personal speculation.	● I can describe what might happen next in a story. ● I can describe how characters change in a story.
Phase ② activities pages 61-62				
Following a sequence Children can understand that a story has a logical sequence of events.	● Paired activity where children complete an interactive sequencing activity, compare two text extracts and record plot and character links. ● Children's discussions and written responses on the completed photocopiable.	**Reading AF2** ● Some specific straightforward information recalled. ● Generally clear idea of where to look for information.	**Reading AF2** ● Simple, most obvious points identified though there may also be some misunderstanding. ● Some comments include quotations from or references to text, but not always relevant.	I can identify events in a story.

Unit 4 ⬜ Extended stories/Significant authors

Learning outcomes	Assessment opportunity and evidence	Assessment focuses (AFs)		Success criteria
		Level 2	**Level 3**	
Making a storyboard Children can plan a story that has a logical sequence of events.	• Paired activity where children plan their own story. • Children's discussions and their pictorial storyboards.	**Writing AF3** • Some basic sequencing of ideas or material. • Openings and/or closings sometimes signalled.	**Writing AF3** • Some attempt to organise ideas with related points placed next to each other. • Openings and closings usually signalled. • Some attempt to sequence ideas or material logically.	• I can plan and write a complete story. • I can plan a story that has a sequence of events.

Phase ③ activities pages 62-63

Working in a group Children can work as a member of a group to present a scene from a known story to an audience.	• Paired and group activity where children freeze-frame a key moment from a story and plan a dramatisation of it. • Teacher observation and group interaction. • Children's completed self-assessment of their group work.	**Reading AF6** • Some awareness that writers have viewpoints and purposes. • Simple statements about likes and dislikes in reading, sometimes with reasons.	**Reading AF6** • Comments identify main purpose. • Express personal response but with little awareness of writer's viewpoint or effect on reader.	I can work with a group to plan and present a drama.
Improving presentation Children can respond to presentations by making constructive comments.	• Group activity where children present their dramatisation to the class and the audience review the performances. • Teacher observation and group performances. • Children's completed performance reviews.	**Writing AF1** • Mostly relevant ideas and content, sometimes repetitive or sparse. • Some apt word choices create interest. • Brief comments, questions about events or actions suggest viewpoint.	**Writing AF1** • Some appropriate ideas and content included. • Some attempt to elaborate on basic information or events. • Attempt to adopt viewpoint, though often not maintained or inconsistent.	• I can work with a group to plan and present a drama. • I can comment on the presentations of others.

Phase ① Understanding the story opening

Learning outcome
Children can make predictions about a text and discuss the way characters develop across a story.

Success criteria
- I can describe what might happen next in a story.
- I can describe how characters change in a story.

Setting the context
Prior to this assessment, ensure the children have had experience of stories in which the opening part answers the 'wh-' questions: *Who? What? Where? When? Why?* Display and read the photocopiable page 'The Worst Witch Saves the Day' (extract 1) with the children. Explain that this extract is taken from the opening part of the book so it should answer important 'wh-' questions.

Assessment opportunity
In pairs, ask the children to make a list of all the 'wh-' question words that they can think of and write these on their individual whiteboards. Ask them to show you these, so that you can check their understanding. Next, give pairs the interactive activity 'Answering wh- questions' to complete. Afterwards, ask the children to read the text again and then discuss with their partners what they have learned about Mildred. Ask everyone to pretend to be Mildred and tell a partner what they are thinking. Then, invite the children to draw a picture of Mildred and surround the image with four thought bubbles. Inside each bubble, ask the children to write a thought that Mildred might have at this early stage in the story.

Assessment evidence
At level 1, the children will benefit from just working on the first half of the text and having it read to them more than once. They will cope with role play and improvised dialogue, but they may manage only short pieces of writing that are not always relevant. At levels 2–3, the children's role play and improvised dialogue will be realistic. They should write interesting and relevant thoughts for Mildred. This activity will provide evidence towards Reading AF2 and Writing AF7.

Next steps
Support: If the children struggle with writing Mildred's thoughts, make an assessment on oral dialogue.
Extension: Suggest the children add two more thoughts to Mildred's head and speak all the thoughts to a listening partner for the partner to assess their realism.

Key aspects of learning
Communication: Children will develop their ability to discuss as they work collaboratively in paired, group and whole-class contexts. They will communicate outcomes orally, in writing and through ICT if appropriate.

NARRATIVE

Phase ① Making predictions

Learning outcome
Children can make predictions about a text and discuss the way characters develop across a story.

Success criteria
● I can describe what might happen next in a story.
● I can describe how characters change in a story.

Setting the context
The children should have already discussed characters in stories and understand that we can learn what a character is like from the things that they say and do. Ensure the children have already completed the previous activity and have their notes on Mildred to hand. Explain that you are now going to read a second extract from the same story. Display the photocopiable page 'The Worst Witch Saves the Day' (extract 2) and read it together.

Assessment opportunity
In pairs, ask the children to discuss what happens in the extract. As with the previous activity, ask them to role play Mildred, thinking and feeling as she does during the scene. Provide the children with paper to record four fresh thought bubbles for Mildred. Then, invite them to compare these thought bubbles with their work from the previous activity, to decide if and how the author has changed and developed the character. Next, ask the children to imagine that they are the author and must plan what will happen next in the story. Suggest they try out ideas using role play and improvised dialogue with a partner, before they complete the photocopiable page 'Extending the story'.

Assessment evidence
At level 1, the children should speak simple thoughts to a partner and their inferences will be on a very basic level. At levels 2–3, the children will make simple but plausible predictions about Mildred's thoughts and actions. This activity will provide evidence towards Reading AF3.

Next steps
Support: If children struggle with the photocopiable page, read the questions aloud to them and concentrate on oral and pictorial answers.
Extension: Suggest the children consider the character of Maud. What have they learned about her so far? If they were the writer, how would they develop this character?

Key aspects of learning
Communication: Children will develop their ability to discuss as they work collaboratively in paired, group and whole-class contexts. They will communicate outcomes orally, in writing and through ICT if appropriate.

Phase ② Following a sequence

Learning outcome
Children can understand that a story has a logical sequence of events.

Success criteria
I can identify events in a story.

Setting the context
Ensure the children have already read the two extracts from *The Worst Witch Saves the Day* (see the previous Phase 1 activities). Display the extracts and discuss, as a class, what happened in the two scenes.

Assessment opportunity
Remind the children that events in a story should follow a logical sequence. Assess their grasp of this by giving pairs of children the interactive activity 'Follow the sequence'. To complete this, children must put the story events in the correct order. Afterwards, display and read the photocopiable page 'The Worst Witch Saves the Day' (extract 3). Give the children copies of this text and a copy of the photocopiable page 'The Worst Witch Saves the Day' (extract 2). Suggest that they re-read both extracts with a partner before completing the photocopiable page 'Finding links'.

Assessment evidence
At level 1, the children may make initial errors when sequencing the story events. Their answers on the photocopiable page 'Finding links' may be entirely pictorial. At levels 2–3, the children will complete the interactive activity with more certainty. They will identify links between the extracts with more assurance and complete the photocopiable page using writing and pictures. This activity will provide evidence towards Reading AF2.

Next steps
Support: If the children struggle with recording on the photocopiable page, suggest they indicate their answers by highlighting matching links on the two extracts.
Extension: Let partners discuss the author's links in these extracts. Challenge them to suggest another link that the author could have written.

Key aspects of learning
Communication: Children will develop their ability to discuss as they work collaboratively in paired, group and whole-class contexts. They will communicate outcomes orally, in writing and through ICT if appropriate.

Phase ② Making a storyboard

Learning outcome
Children can plan a story that has a logical sequence of events.

Success criteria
● I can plan and write a complete story.
● I can plan a story that has a sequence of events.

Setting the context
Ensure the children have read complete stories and have recognised that a good story needs four key ingredients: characters, setting, events in a logical sequence and an ending. Write these as headings on the whiteboard. Explain to the children that they will eventually be writing their own stories. In order to start planning their story, they must decide on their choice for each of the four key ingredients.

Assessment opportunity
Put the children into pairs to discuss their story ideas and match them to the key ingredients. If necessary, provide children with the photocopiable page, 'Picture prompts', to help them decide on characters, settings, events and a possible ending.

Afterwards, ask the children to create a pictorial plan of their story using four boxes, one for each key ingredient.

Assessment evidence
At level 1, the children will probably use the picture prompts for their storyboard, may only plan two key events and need advice on an ending. At levels 2–3, the children will often have independent story ideas and should be able to complete all the boxes. This activity will provide evidence towards Writing AF3.

Next steps
Support: If children struggle with the task, let them supply oral answers to you first, before going on to complete the storyboard.
Extension: Suggest the children do a self-assessment of their work.

Key aspects of learning
Self-awareness: As they work on an extended piece of writing, children will learn how to organise their own work and how to maintain their concentration to complete a polished story.

Phase ③ Working in a group

Learning outcome
Children can work as a member of a group to present a scene from a known story to an audience.

Success criteria
I can work with a group to plan and present a drama.

Setting the context
Ensure the children have experience of identifying key moments in a story and of doing drama presentations for an audience. They should have already read the photocopiable page 'The Worst Witch Saves the Day' (extract 2). Give the children a copy of the extract. Ask them to re-read it in pairs and decide on its key moment.

Assessment opportunity
Challenge the children to show the key moment as a freeze-frame. Discover which part of the text the pairs have identified by questioning children while they pose in character. Return the children's pictorial storyboards from the previous activity. Ask everyone to decide on a key moment in their story and tell their partner about it. Then, put the children into groups of four to compare their key moments. Challenge each group to choose one key moment to perform as a drama to the rest of the class. Allow rehearsal time for the groups to prepare their dramatisation, observing how they allocate parts and make decisions about who says what and when. Suggest they use improvised dialogue rather than rehearsing lines. Afterwards, give everyone the photocopiable page 'Working together on a drama' to complete.

Assessment evidence
At level 1, the children may need help in organising the reporting of key moments when groups of four are formed. They should be guided towards making a wise choice for their production. At levels 2–3, the children will be able to report key moments to their group, but may need reminding to choose the one that has the most dramatic appeal. They should have more interesting and thoughtful answers on their completed photocopiable. This activity will provide evidence towards Reading AF6.

Next steps
Support: If children struggle with their rehearsals, offer adult support or reduce the task to creating a sequence of freeze-frames, one of which is identified as the key moment.
Extension: Suggest the children write an explanation of how their group will act out their drama.

> **Key aspects of learning**
> **Communication:** Children will develop their ability to discuss as they work collaboratively in paired, group and whole-class contexts. They will communicate outcomes orally, in writing and through ICT if appropriate.

Phase ③ Improving presentation

Learning outcome
Children can respond to presentations by making constructive comments.

Success criteria
- I can work with a group to plan and present a drama.
- I can comment on the presentations of others.

Setting the context
Ensure the children have completed the previous activity and have experience of commenting constructively on a peer's work. Return the children's completed photocopiable page 'Working together on a drama' (from the previous activity). Put the children back into the same groups of four to revise and rehearse their presentation.

Assessment opportunity
Explain that the class will watch and review each of the group presentations. Provide everyone with the photocopiable page 'Theatre critic'. After each presentation, ask the audience to review the performance by adding their comments to the photocopiable page.

Assessment evidence
At level 1, the children's dramatisation may be short and need guidance from you, but children in the acting group should be helpful to one another. Their review comments will be brief or pictorial. At levels 2–3, the children will work well in a group and support one another within their dramatisation. Their review comments should be interesting and often constructive. This activity will provide evidence towards Writing AF1.

Next steps
Support: If children struggle with writing review notes, suggest they talk to a partner first, and then record their thoughts pictorially.
Extension: Suggest the children write review notes for their own group's dramatisation. Afterwards, let them compare review notes with a partner. Ask the children if they think they identified key moments as their highlights.

Key aspects of learning
Evaluation: Children will discuss success criteria for their written work, give feedback to others and judge the quality of their own writing.
Communication: Children will develop their ability to discuss as they work collaboratively in paired, group and whole-class contexts. They will communicate outcomes orally, in writing and through ICT if appropriate.

NARRATIVE

Periodic assessment

Reading

Learning outcomes
- Children can plan a story that has a logical sequence of events.
- Children can work as a member of a group to present a scene from a known story to an audience.

Success criteria
- I can describe what might happen in a story.
- I can identify events in a story.
- I can work with a group to plan and present a drama.

Setting the context
Children should have had experience of reading a whole story and discussing the characters and events that comprise that story. Display and re-read the photocopiable page 'The Worst Witch Saves the Day' (extract 3) from the Phase 2 activity 'Following a sequence'. Give the children individual copies of the text and put them into small groups of comparable ability.

Assessment opportunity
Ask the children to discuss the extract in their groups. Assess understanding of the events and characters by observing and listening to the discussions. Invite each group to perform the events, with you as their audience. As a follow-up, ask the children to think about what might happen next in the story. Let them record their predictions in three or four storyboard pictures, adding a sentence beneath each picture.

Assessment evidence
At level 1, the children will enact the scene correctly, but may need reminding of their own role. Their storyboard may have only one or two pictures and no writing. At levels 2–3, the children will hold more interesting discussions and their presentation will be more animated. Their storyboard should have two or three pictures and some sentences. This activity will help you judge the children's overall understanding of work in this unit and provide evidence against Reading AF2, AF3 and AF6.

SCHOLASTIC

Periodic assessment

Writing

Learning outcomes
- Children can plan a story that has a logical sequence of events.
- Children can write an extended narrative with:
  - a logical sequence of events;
  - sentences grouped together;
  - temporal connectives;
  - consistent use of the third person and past tense.

Success criteria
I can plan and write a complete story that has a logical sequence of events.

Setting the context
Return the children's pictorial storyboards from the Phase 2 activity, 'Making a storyboard'.

Assessment opportunity
Put the children working at level 1 into pairs and ask them to retell their stories to each other, using their plans as a prompt. Suggest to the children working at levels 2–3 that they need to extend their storyboard plans with more detailed written notes. Provide them with sheets of paper, displaying the four key headings: 'opening', 'something happens', 'events to sort it out' and 'ending'. Ask them to write notes under each relevant heading to supplement their pictorial storyboard. Afterwards, offer the children the option of writing their extended story on paper or on screen, adding illustrations if they wish. Allow them plenty of time to write their stories.

Assessment evidence
At level 1, the children may need help remembering their storyboard plans, but should be able to tell their story to a partner. When writing their story, they may fail to include all the parts of their plan. At levels 2–3, the children should make useful written notes on the photocopiable 'Story planner' (see Unit 1, Phase 3 activity 'Story planning'). They will write a longer story and will include most of the points on their plan. This activity will help you judge the children's overall understanding of work in this unit and will provide evidence against Writing AF1, AF3, AF7 and AF8.

NARRATIVE

THE
Worst Witch
SAVES THE DAY

(Extract 1)

"This is just typical!" thought Mildred Hubble, wriggling her toes uncomfortably inside thick grey socks and heavy winter boots. "When we came back for Summer Term it was snowing and we were all frozen to death in our summer dresses!"

Mildred was beginning her third year at Miss Cackle's Academy. She was relieved to be coming back at all, after an accident-prone two years under the beady eye of the blood-curdling Miss Hardbroom (or H.B. as the girls called her), who had been Mildred's form-mistress for both of those years. However, this term Mildred felt much more confident. During the summer break, she had been on a special two-week broomstick crash course (a rather unfortunate description in Mildred's case) and had received a Broomstick Proficiency

Certificate and a smart new broom from her mum as a reward. Sadly, her cat, Tabby, who was the only tabby cat in the school (all the rest being regulation black ones), had not improved very much – in fact, at *all*, if one was to be truthful.

Text and illustration © 2005 Jill Murphy

Name	Date

Extending the story

What two new pieces of information have you found out about Mildred?

1. _____

2. _____

In what two ways has the story moved on?

1. _____

2. _____

Draw a picture to show what might happen next in the story.

[ ]

Write a sentence about your picture.

_____

_____

Red
Amber
Green

I can describe what might happen next in a story. ☐

I can describe how characters change in a story. ☐

NON-FICTION
UNIT 1 Instructions

Literacy objectives

Speak and listen for a wide range of purposes in different contexts
Strand 1 Speaking
- Speak with clarity and use appropriate intonation when reading and reciting texts.

Strand 2 Listening and responding
- Listen to others in class, ask relevant questions and follow instructions.

Read and write for a range of purposes on paper and on screen
Strand 5 Word recognition: decoding (reading) and encoding (spelling)
- Read independently and with increasing fluency longer and less familiar texts.
- Spell with increasing accuracy and confidence, drawing on word recognition and knowledge of word structure, and spelling patterns.
- Know how to tackle unfamiliar words that are not completely decodable.
- Read and spell less common alternative graphemes including trigraphs.
- Read high and medium frequency words independently and automatically.

Strand 6 Word structure and spelling
- Spell with increasing accuracy and confidence, drawing on word recognition and knowledge of word structure, and spelling patterns including common inflections and use of double letters.
- Read and spell less common alternative graphemes including trigraphs.

Strand 7 Understanding and interpreting texts
- Give some reasons why things happen or characters change.
- Explain organisational features of texts, including alphabetical order, layout, diagrams, captions, hyperlinks and bullet points.

Strand 8 Engaging with and responding to texts
- Engage with books through exploring and enacting interpretations.

Strand 9 Creating and shaping texts
- Draw on knowledge and experience of texts in deciding and planning what and how to write.
- Maintain consistency in non-narrative, including purpose and tense.
- Select from different presentational features to suit particular writing purposes on paper and on screen.

Strand 10 Text structure and organisation
- Use appropriate language to make sections hang together.

Strand 11 Sentence structure and punctuation
- Use question marks, and use commas to separate items in a list.

Unit 1 ☐ **Instructions**

Key aspects of learning

Enquiry
- Children will ask questions arising from work in another area of the curriculum, for example questions about planting beans.

Reasoning
- Children will sequence actions logically to form a set of instructions.

Evaluation
- Children will give instructions orally and in writing. They will judge the effectiveness of their own work.

Social skills
- When working collaboratively, children will learn about listening to and respecting other people's contributions.

Communication
- Children will develop their ability to discuss as they work collaboratively in paired, group and whole-class contexts. They will communicate outcomes orally, in writing and through ICT if appropriate.

Assessment focuses

Reading

AF2 *(understand, describe, select or retrieve information, events or ideas from texts and use quotation and reference to text).*
AF5 *(explain and comment on writers' use of language, including grammatical and literary features at word and sentence level).*

Writing

AF2 *(produce texts which are appropriate to task, reader and purpose).*
AF3 *(organise and present whole texts effectively, sequencing and structuring information, ideas and events).*
AF7 *(select appropriate and effective vocabulary).*

Speaking and listening

Speaking (speak with clarity, intonation and pace).
Listening and responding (listen to others; ask relevant questions; follow instructions).

Resources

Phase 1 activities
Photocopiable page, 'Giving instructions'
Phase 2 activities
Interactive activity, 'Giving instructions'
Photocopiable page, 'How I got on'
Phase 3 activities
Photocopiable page, 'Three stars and a wish'
Photocopiable page, 'How to produce a white rabbit'
Periodic assessment
Interactive activity, 'Non-fiction 1 Reading assessment (a)'
Photocopiable page, 'Non-fiction 1 Reading assessment (b)
Photocopiable page, Non-fiction 1 Reading assessment (c)
Photocopiable page, 'Non-fiction 1 Writing assessment'

Unit 1 📖 Instructions

Learning outcomes	Assessment opportunity and evidence	Assessment focuses (AFs)	Success criteria
		Level 1	
Phase ① activities pages 73–74			
Listening to instructions Children can follow a series of simple instructions correctly.	● Group activity where children demonstrate their listening and retention skills by responding to a series of instructions. ● Children's responses to oral instructions.	**Reading AF2** ● Some simple points from familar texts recalled ● Some pages/sections of interest located.	I can listen to and follow simple instructions.
Giving and testing instructions Children can effectively give oral instructions in the correct sequence.	● Paired and group activity where children discuss and plan their own PE activity, before taking it in turns to give and follow oral instructions. ● Partner planning and discussion, followed by testing of instructions. ● Children's written self-assessments.	**Writing AF2** Some indication of basic purpose, particular form or awareness of reader.	● I can test and give oral instructions. ● I can give oral instructions in the correct order.
Phase ② activities pages 75–76			
Saying and writing instructions Children can write a series of instructions.	● Paired and group activity where children recognise instructional sentences and use imperative verbs to give instructions. ● Children's participation in the oral game and delivery of instructions to their partner. ● Children's written lists of instructions.	**Writing AF7** ● Mostly simple vocabulary. ● Communicates meaning through repetition of key words.	I can say and write instructions.
Using two forms of instruction Children can write instructions in two forms.	● Paired activity where children match different forms of instruction and self-assess their understanding of the two forms of instruction. ● Partner discussion and completion of the interactive activity. ● Children's oral answers when playing the partner game, and written self-assessment.	**Reading AF5** Comments on obvious features of language.	I can say and write instructions by giving an order and by describing a process.

Unit 1 📖 Instructions

Learning outcomes	Assessment opportunity and evidence	Assessment focuses (AFs) Level 1	Success criteria

Phase ③ activities pages 77–78

Learning outcomes	Assessment opportunity and evidence	Assessment focuses (AFs) Level 1	Success criteria
Testing instructions Children can say a simple sequence of instructions to be followed by another child.	● Paired activity where children plan and rehearse instructions for a simple art activity, which are given orally to a partner to perform and assess the effectiveness of the instructions. ● Children rehearse and give oral instructions to a partner. ● Children's written peer-assessment.	**Writing AF3** ● Some formulaic phrases indicate start/end of text. ● Events/ideas sometimes in appropriate order.	● I can give clear instructions. ● I can evaluate oral instructions.
Making a checklist Children can write a simple sequence of instructions to be followed by another child or group.	● Paired activity where children read an instruction text, identify the important features of written instructions and list them in a checklist. ● Discussion of the instruction text. ● Children's written notes and checklists.	**Writing AF2** Some indication of basic purpose, particular form or awareness of reader.	I can write a checklist to help other people to write instructions.

Learning outcomes	Assessment opportunity and evidence	Assessment focuses (AFs)		Success criteria
		Level 2	Level 3	

Phase ① activities pages 73–74

Learning outcomes	Assessment opportunity and evidence	Level 2	Level 3	Success criteria
Listening to instructions Children can follow a series of simple instructions correctly.	● Group activity where children demonstrate their listening and retention skills by responding to a series of instructions. ● Children's responses to oral instructions.	**Reading AF2** ● Some specific, straighforward information recalled. ● Generally clear idea of where to look for information.	**Reading AF2** ● Simple, most obvious points identified though there may also be some misunderstanding. ● Some comments include quotations from or references to text, but not always relevant.	I can listen to and follow simple instructions.
Giving and testing instructions Children can effectively give oral instructions in the correct sequence.	● Paired and group activity where children discuss and plan their own PE activity, before taking it in turns to give and follow oral instructions. ● Partner planning and discussion, followed by testing of instructions. ● Children's written self-assessments.	**Writing AF2** ● Some basic Purpose established. ● Some appropriate features of the given form used. ● Some attempts to adopt appropriate style.	**Writing AF2** ● Purpose established at a general level. ● Main features of selected form sometimes signalled to the reader. ● Some attempts at appropriate style, with attention to reader.	● I can test and give oral instructions. ● I can give oral instructions in the correct order.

Unit 1 Instructions

Learning outcomes	Assessment opportunity and evidence	Assessment focuses (AFs)		Success criteria
		Level 2	Level 3	
Phase ② activities pages 75–76				
Saying and writing instructions Children can write a series of instructions.	• Paired and group activity where children recognise instructional sentences and use imperative verbs to give instructions. • Children's participation in the oral game and delivery of instructions to their partner. • Children's written lists of instructions.	**Writing AF7** • Simple, often speech-like vocabulary conveys relevant meanings. • Some adventurous word choices.	**Writing AF7** • Simple generally appropriate vocabulary used, limited in range. • Some words selected for effect or occasion.	I can say and write instructions.
Using two forms of instruction Children can write instructions in two forms.	• Independent and paired activity where children match different forms of instruction and self-assess their understanding of the two forms of instruction. • Partner discussion and independent completion of the interactive activity. • Children's oral answers when playing the partner game, and written self-assessment.	**Reading AF5** • Some effective language choices noted. • Some familiar patterns of language identified.	**Reading AF5** A few basic features of writer's language identified, but with little or no comment.	I can say and write instructions by giving an order and by describing a process.
Phase ③ activities pages 77–78				
Testing instructions Children can say a simple sequence of instructions to be followed by another child.	• Paired activity where children plan and rehearse instructions for a simple art activity, which are given orally to a partner to perform and assess the effectiveness of the instructions. • Children rehearse and give oral instructions to a partner. • Children's written peer-assessment.	**Writing AF3** • Some basic sequencing of ideas or material. • Openings and/or closings sometimes signalled.	**Writing AF3** • Some attempt to organise ideas with related points placed next to each other. • Openings and closings usually signalled. • Some attempt to sequence ideas or material logically.	• I can give clear instructions. • I can evaluate oral instructions.
Making a checklist Children can write a simple sequence of instructions to be followed by another child or group.	• Independent and paired activity where children read an instruction text, identify the important features of written instructions and list them in a checklist. • Discussion of the instruction text. • Children's written notes and checklists.	**Writing AF2** • Some basic purpose established. • Some appropriate features of the given form used. • Some attempts to adopt appropriate style.	**Writing AF2** • Purpose established at a general level. • Main features of selected form sometimes signalled to the reader. • Some attempts at appropriate style, with attention to reader.	I can write a checklist to help other people to write instructions.

Phase ① Listening to instructions

Learning outcome
Children can follow a series of simple instructions correctly.

Success criteria
I can listen to and follow simple instructions.

Setting the context
Ensure the children have experience of following a series of instructions. For this assessment, you will need a large space for the children to move around freely – either the school hall or outdoor area – and a box of ropes.

Assessment opportunity
Perform this activity in small groups, so you can readily observe individual children. Explain to the children that they are going to do a PE activity to improve their balance. Watch carefully as you begin with single warm-up instructions, such as: *Walk on the spot.* Then move on to pairs of instructions. For example: *Find a space and sit on the floor.* Progress to instructions that follow a sequence: *Collect a rope from the box and go back to your place. Spread your rope into a straight line and stand up.* Make your final series of instructions quite complicated: *Start at one end of your rope and walk along it once both ways. After that, choose another person near you. Join your lines together. Play 'Follow my leader' and walk down your new line. Walk once in both directions. After that, change leader.* Let the children stop you to ask questions, but keep returning to your sequence of instructions. Repeat the activity to assess if children's listening skills and language retention improves.

Assessment evidence
At level 1, the children should recall the single instructions, but may have to have pairs of instructions repeated to them. With the final sequence of instructions, they are likely to forget what to do or will start doing things in the wrong order. At levels 2–3, the children will recall confidently the single and paired instructions. For the final sequence of instructions, they may confer with their partner or ask you for confirmation of some of the sequence. This activity will provide evidence towards Reading AF2.

Next steps
Support: If the children struggle with the later stage, repeat an instruction more slowly, often saying only half of the sentence at a time.
Extension: Suggest the children discuss the activity and your use of language with their partner.

Key aspects of learning
Social skills: When working collaboratively, children will learn about listening to and respecting other people's contributions.
Communication: Children will develop their ability to discuss as they work collaboratively in paired, group and whole-class contexts. They will communicate outcomes orally, in writing and through ICT if appropriate.

NON-FICTION

Phase ① Giving and testing instructions

Learning outcome
Children can effectively give oral instructions in the correct sequence.

Success criteria
● I can test and give oral instructions.
● I can give oral instructions in the correct order.

Setting the context
Ensure the children have already completed the previous activity. Do this assessment with small groups of about eight children of comparable ability. Ensure there is ample space, so you can readily hear and observe the children as they perform the task.

Assessment opportunity
Put the children into pairs. Remind them of the previous activity, explaining that you want them to think of a new, short, balance game using a rope. If the children are stuck for ideas, suggest new movements or changes of direction. Give pairs time to discuss and decide on a game before you put the pairs into groups of four. Give each group two short ropes. Ask one pair to give instructions, while the other two children follow them. Then let pairs swap roles. Suggest each pair has a second try at giving instructions, so that they have the chance to improve. As you observe, assess how well speakers give their instructions. Afterwards, give the children their own copy of the self-assessment photocopiable page 'Giving instructions' to complete. Support children working at level 1 in recording some of their answers.

Assessment evidence
At level 1, the children may only give two or three instructions, and they may be similar to yours. They should be able to put them in the correct sequence. At levels 2–3, the children's instructions will number about four. They may make sequence mistakes, but should identify most of these, and make improvements with their second try. Use the children's self-assessment to provide evidence towards Writing AF2.

Next steps
Support: If the children struggle to think of their own game, provide a simple idea with two or three clear stages.
Extension: Suggest the children compare their completed photocopiables. Let them test their ideas for improving their oral instructions by instructing each other.

Key aspects of learning
Reasoning: Children will sequence actions logically to form a set of instructions.
Evaluation: Children will give instructions orally and in writing. They will judge the effectiveness of their own work.
Communication: Children will develop their ability to discuss as they work collaboratively in paired, group and whole-class contexts. They will communicate outcomes orally, in writing and through ICT if appropriate.

Phase ② Saying and writing instructions

NON-FICTION

Learning outcome
Children can write a series of instructions.

Success criteria
I can say and write instructions.

Setting the context
Ensure the children have experience of listening to and giving an instruction. Perform this assessment in small groups so you can readily hear and observe individuals.

Assessment opportunity
Tell the children that it is time for a game. Explain that the game is called 'I'm the boss!' and is similar to 'Simon says...'. The rule of the game is to do only what you are told. Demonstrate by giving the children a few instructions involving simple actions for them to obey. For example, *Give a thumbs-up sign, tap your feet, hop on your left leg*, and so on. Put the children into pairs to continue to play the game, each child taking turns to give three instructions. Emphasise that the listener must only obey when the speaker gives a proper instruction. Encourage the children to progress to instructions for simple classroom procedures. For example, *walking across the room and collecting a book*. Suggest the children keep count of how many successful instructions they hear and obey. Ask the children to write five instructions that they made. Retain the children's written lists.

Assessment evidence
At level 1, the children may deviate from imperative verbs and will need reminding that only instructions will be obeyed. They should manage to write, with some support, two instructions. At levels 2–3, the children will be more confident in their use of imperative verbs to form an instruction. They should write independently a few correct instructions. This activity will provide evidence towards Writing AF7.

Next steps
Support: If children struggle with writing, let them say their instruction and you record it for them to copy.
Extension: Suggest the children extend their written lists, adding two sets of four consecutive instructions for classroom procedures.

Key aspects of learning
Evaluation: Children will give instructions orally and in writing. They will judge the effectiveness of their own work.
Communication: Children will develop their ability to discuss as they work collaboratively in paired, group and whole-class contexts. They will communicate outcomes orally, in writing and through ICT if appropriate.

Phase ② Using two forms of instruction

Learning outcome
Children can write instructions in two forms.

Success criteria
I can say and write instructions by giving an order and by describing a process.

Setting the context
Ensure the children have had experience of pairs of instructions, in which one form gives an order and the other describes a process. They should have discussed the language features of these forms and have used the term 'imperative'.

Assessment opportunity
Remind the children that there are two ways to give an instruction. Revise this by giving them the interactive activity 'Giving instructions' to complete. Children working at level 1 should do this with a partner. Suggest the children print their results afterwards and discuss the matched sentences in groups or with their partner. Listen as they make observations about similarities and differences in the instructions. Challenge the children to identify, write on their individual whiteboard and hold up the word that appears in the longer instruction but is not used in its matched shorter form 'You'. Ask them to identify, write and hold up an imperative verb. What do the children notice about imperative verbs and short instructions? Let partners play the 'Say it again' game in which one of them reads an instruction aloud and their partner must say the same instruction in its other form. If correct, they win a point. Then they swap roles. Afterwards, give the children the self-assessment photocopiable page 'How I got on' to complete.

Assessment evidence
At level 1, the children will manage the interactive activity, although they may need it to be read aloud. Their partner discussion will be less observant and they may not identify the features asked for. They will play the game with some success. At levels 2–3, the children will complete the interactive activity independently and make perceptive comments about the structure of the two forms. This activity will provide evidence towards Reading AF5.

Next steps
Support: If the children struggle with reading for the oral game, let an adult provide the longer form of the instruction and the children say the shorter form.
Extension: Suggest the children revisit their written instructions from the previous activity and write an alternative form for each.

Key aspects of learning
Evaluation: Children will give instructions orally and in writing. They will judge the effectiveness of their own work.
Social skills: When working collaboratively, children will learn about listening to and respecting other people's contributions.
Communication: Children will develop their ability to discuss as they work collaboratively in paired, group and whole-class contexts. They will communicate outcomes orally, in writing and through ICT if appropriate.

Phase ③ Testing instructions

Learning outcome
Children can say a simple sequence of instructions to be followed by another child.

Success criteria
- I can give clear instructions.
- I can evaluate oral instructions.

Setting the context
Ensure the children have already had experience of giving and following sequential, oral instructions. For this assessment, choose a simple art activity that the children are familiar with, such as making a greetings card in a particular shape (a Christmas tree or an Easter egg). Refresh the children's memories by demonstrating with a sheet of paper how you usually make this type of card. Ask the children to imagine that another child does not know how to make this card, so they must give them clear, oral instructions.

Assessment opportunity
Suggest to the children that they rehearse their instructions independently, saying oral instructions to themselves as they pretend to fold, draw and cut a piece of paper. Then put them into pairs of comparable ability, giving each child an appropriate piece of paper. Let each partner take a turn being the instructor, while the other follows the instructions and makes a card. Encourage partners to point out to their instructor if and when an oral instruction is not clear and needs changing. Afterwards, give everyone the peer-assessment photocopiable page 'Three stars and a wish' to complete.

Assessment evidence
At level 1, the children's oral instructions may only have a few steps and their order may be muddled. Partner reactions should help them self-correct. Answers on the photocopiable will be brief and you may need to read questions aloud to them and prompt ideas. At levels 2–3, the children will give instructions more confidently. They will quickly recognise mistakes and self-correct after partner reaction. Their comments on the photocopiable page should be perceptive. This activity will provide evidence towards Writing AF3.

Next steps
Support: If children struggle with the photocopiable page, read the questions aloud and record their answers.
Extension: Suggest the children use the same 'Three stars and a wish' format to make a self-assessment of their own oral instructions and compare it with the assessment made by their partner.

Key aspects of learning
Reasoning: Children will sequence actions logically to form a set of instructions.
Evaluation: Children will give instructions orally and in writing. They will judge the effectiveness of their own work.

Phase ③ Making a checklist

Success criteria
I can write a checklist to help other people to write instructions.

Setting the context
Prior to this assessment, ensure the children have had experience of reading and following instructions, and are aware of the conventional linguistic and organisational features in written instructions. Display an enlarged version of the photocopiable page 'How to produce a white rabbit'. Read it aloud and then ask the children to comment on the type of text they think it is. Give the children individual copies of the text to read and discuss with their partners. Explain that you want them to use the text to think about the language and layout features that are important in any written instructions. Suggest they use the text to help them comment on and make brief notes about the important features, highlighting the text if they wish. Use leading questions to draw out answers and help them to notice the important features. Encourage them to highlight relevant parts of the text. Afterwards, explain that you want everyone to use the text to help them create a checklist that instructs children of the important things to remember when writing instructions. Suggest making a checklist of about six to eight points.

Assessment opportunity
While the children are writing their checklists, check whether they are using any of the text-type features of instructions, for example, numbering or bullet points and use of imperative verbs. Have they included a 'How to' title, such as, 'How to write instructions'? At level 1, the children can work with a partner.

Assessment evidence
At level 1, the children's written checklists may only contain a few appropriate language and presentational features. At levels 2–3, the children should produce a list of five or six points and they may manage to sustain an appropriate style throughout some of their writing. This activity will provide evidence towards Writing AF2.

Next steps
Support: If the children struggle on their own, suggest they work with a partner of comparable ability and use their highlighting to help them write a list.
Extension: Challenge the children to provide a checklist of eight points and to give examples from the text of where each point is used.

Key aspects of learning
Social skills: When working collaboratively, children will learn about listening to and respecting other people's contributions.
Communication: Children will develop their ability to discuss as they work collaboratively in paired, group and whole-class contexts. They will communicate outcomes orally, in writing and through ICT if appropriate.

Periodic assessment

Reading

Learning outcome
Children can read and follow a simple sequence of instructions related to another curriculum area or classroom procedure.

Success criteria
- I can follow different types of instructions.
- I can identify what makes instructions easier to follow.
- I can identify how instructions can be improved.

Setting the context
Prior to this assessment, the children should have had experience of reading and following instructions. They should also have identified features that make instructions easier to follow.

Assessment opportunity
Give the children the interactive activity 'Non-fiction 1 Reading assessment (a)' to complete. Children working at level 1 should do this in pairs. Afterwards, get them to print the re-ordered instructions and then use the photocopiable page 'Non-fiction 1 Reading assessment (b)' to tick off features on the list that they can identify in the text. (Warn them that not all the points on the checklist are covered.) Ask them to use the line beneath each item that they have ticked on the checklist to quote an example from the text or to refer to a particular part. Assess the children's comprehension by letting them follow the instructions. Afterwards, give them the photocopiable page 'Non-fiction 1 Reading assessment (c)' to complete.

Assessment evidence
At level 1, the children will prefer to do all the activities in pairs, relying on each other and an adult for support in reading some words and confirming their judgement. When completing the photocopiable page 'Non-fiction 1 Reading assessment (c)', they may fail to recognise the relevance of the boxes they did not tick on their 'Checklist for instructions'. At levels 2–3, the children will complete the interactive activity independently, but may benefit from partner discussion when completing the photocopiable pages and putting the instructions 'How to do a scraffito picture' into practice. This activity will help you judge the children's overall understanding of work in this unit and provide evidence against Reading AF4 and AF5.

Periodic assessment

Writing

Learning outcome
Children can write a simple sequence of instructions to be followed by another child or group.

Success criteria
- I can say and write instructions.
- I can plan and edit my instructions.
- I can include sequence words and diagrams.

Setting the context
Ensure the children have already done the periodic reading activity and have made a personal checklist of important features of instructional texts (see Phase 3 activity, 'Making a checklist').

Assessment opportunity
Provide the children with the photocopiable page 'Non-fiction 1 Writing assessment'. Remind them that these instructions are not in the correct sequence and that they could be improved. Return the children's completed photocopiable page 'Non-fiction 1 Reading assessment (c)' (from the Periodic Reading activity) so that they can remind themselves of the improvements they planned. Let them discuss their ideas with a partner. Give out scissors, paper and glue and invite the children to cut out the sections of the photocopiable page 'Non-fiction 1 Writing assessment', sort them into a logical sequence and then stick them onto the paper. Afterwards, they will need to make the additions they planned in the periodic reading activity and, if needed, make a final neat copy of the improved instructions.

Assessment evidence
At level 1, the children may need to remind themselves of the correct sequence by doing the interactive activity 'Non-fiction 1 Reading assessment (a)' again. They may need support as they consider their planned improvements from the photocopiable page 'Non-fiction 1 Reading assessment (c)'. They should be able to make some improvements to the final instructions from the photocopiable page 'Non-fiction 1 Writing assessment'. At levels 2–3, the children will readily remember the lack of sequence in the given text. Their improved final text should make considerable improvements to the original text. This activity will help you judge the children's overall understanding of work in this unit and provide evidence against Writing AF2, AF3, and AF7.

How to produce a white rabbit

What you need:

- wizard's coat
- tall spell hat
- magic wand

What to do

1. Put on your wizard's coat and tall spell hat.

2. After that, wave your wand in a large circle.

3. Wait until six white stars appear in the circle.

4. Next chant, "Rabbit-ca-dabra! Rabbit-ca-dabra! Rabbit-ca-dabra!"

5. Carefully take off your hat.

6. Watch a white rabbit hop out!

Illustration © 2010, Anna Godwin/Beehive Illustration.

NON-FICTION
UNIT 2 Explanations

Literacy objectives

Speak and listen for a wide range of purposes in different contexts
Strand 1 Speaking
- Explain ideas and processes using imaginative and adventurous vocabulary and non-verbal gestures to support communication.

Strand 3 Group discussion and interaction
- Ensure that everyone contributes, allocate tasks, and consider alternatives and reach agreement.

Read and write for a range of purposes on paper and on screen
Strand 5 Word recognition: decoding (reading) and encoding (spelling)
- Spell with increasing accuracy and confidence, drawing on word recognition and knowledge of word structure, and spelling patterns.
- Know how to tackle unfamiliar words that are not completely decodable.
- Read high and medium frequency words independently and automatically.
- Read and spell less common alternative graphemes including trigraphs.

Strand 7 Understanding and interpreting texts
- Give some reasons why things happen or characters change.
- Explain organisational features of texts, including alphabetical order, layout, diagrams, captions, hyperlinks and bullet points.

Strand 8 Engaging with and responding to texts
- Engage with books through exploring and enacting interpretations.

Strand 9 Creating and shaping texts
- Draw on knowledge and experience of texts in deciding and planning what and how to write.
- Select from different presentational features to suit particular writing purposes on paper and on screen.

Strand 10 Text structure and organisation
- Use planning to establish clear sections for writing.
- Use appropriate language to make sections hang together.

Strand 11 Sentence structure and punctuation
- Write simple and compound sentences and begin to use subordination in relation to time and reason.

Key aspects of learning

Enquiry
- Children will carry out their own enquiry or investigation in another area of the curriculum, and will make observations and explain what they have found out. Throughout their enquiry, children will be encouraged to pose questions prior to, during and after their investigation. They will decide the most appropriate presentation for their findings.

Information processing
- Children will identify relevant information from observation and practical experience, information texts and ICT texts and select this to help them write their own explanation text for an individual or class book or wall display,

> ## Key aspects of learning (continued)
>
> **Evaluation**
> ● Children will present information orally and in writing, in the form of a flow chart or cyclic diagram. They will be able to support their judgements with their own evidence, drawing on a range of sources to support their evaluation.
> **Communication**
> ● Children will develop their ability to express and communicate in spoken, pictorial and written form a simple explanation of a process. They may also communicate their ideas using a variety of prompts, including models, diagrams and charts.

Assessment focuses

Reading
AF2 (understand, describe, select or retrieve information, events or ideas from texts and use quotation and reference to text).
AF4 (identify and comment on the structure and organisation of texts, including grammatical and presentational features at text level).

Writing
AF2 (produce texts which are appropriate to task, reader and purpose).
AF3 (organise and present whole texts effectively, sequencing and structuring information, ideas and events).
AF7 (select appropriate and effective vocabulary).

Speaking and listening
Speaking (use language and gesture when providing an explanation).
Group discussion and interaction (listen to each other's views and preferences).

Resources

Phase 1 activities
Photocopiable page, 'Key words'
Photocopiable page, 'Using key words'
Photocopiable page, 'Index'
Phase 2 activities
Photocopiable page, 'How do peas grow?'
Photocopiable page, 'Watching an explanation'
Photocopiable page, 'Three stars and a wish'
Phase 3 activities
Interactive activity, 'Finding features'
Photocopiable page, 'How do peas grow?'
Photocopiable page, 'Features of an explanation text' (versions 1 and 2)
Photocopiable page, 'A pictorial flow chart'
Phase 4 activities
Photocopiable page, 'A cyclical flow chart'
Photocopiable page, 'A pictorial flow chart'
Periodic assessment
Photocopiable page, 'Non-fiction 2 Reading assessment text'
Interactive activity, 'Non-fiction 2 Reading assessment (a)'
Photocopiable page, 'Non-fiction 2 Reading assessment (b)'
Photocopiable page, 'Non-fiction 2 Writing assessment'

Unit 2 ⬜ Explanations

Learning outcomes	Assessment opportunity and evidence	Assessment focuses (AFs)	Success criteria
		Level 1	
Phase ① activities pages 87–88			
Identifying key words Children can find a key word using an index and then locate the relevant information on a page.	● Paired activity where children identify key words relating to a topic and then use an index to identify where they would go to find out more information. ● Children's completed photocopiables.	**Reading AF2** ● Some simple points from familiar texts recalled. ● Some pages/sections of interest located.	● I can identify key words. ● I can use an index to find information in a book.
Creating order Children can make and use a glossary of special interest words related to an investigation.	● Group activity where children play a game, putting key words into alphabetical order and then type up their own index using key words from the previous session. ● Children's completed indexes.	**Writing AF2** Some indication of basic purpose, particular form or awareness of reader.	● I can put words in alphabetical order. ● I can make a glossary.
Phase ② activities pages 89–90			
Modelling and explaining Children can model a process using models, pictures and diagrams and explain the process to peers.	● Paired and group activity where children create and present a human flow chart to model the life cycle of a pea and the audience review each presentation. ● Partner discussion. ● Children's completed peer assessments.	**Reading AF4** Some awareness of meaning of simple text features.	● I can explain a process to others using models, pictures and diagrams. ● I can present and evaluate explanations.
Presenting and evaluating Children can model a process using models, pictures and diagrams and explain the process to peers.	● Paired activity where children rehearse and give a presentation of their individual pictorial flow chart and assess their own presentation using the photocopiable. ● Paired rehearsal and individual oral presentations. ● Children's completed self-assessments.	**Writing AF7** ● Mostly simple vocabulary. ● Communicates meaning through repetition of key words.	● I can identify ways of presenting an explanation. ● I can present and evaluate explanations.
Phase ③ activities pages 90–91			
Identifying explanation features Children can recognise the structure and language features of an explanation text.	● Paired activity where children complete an interactive activity, spotting key features of an explanation text and complete the photocopiable to reinforce their learning. ● Children's completed photocopiables.	**Reading AF4** Some awareness of meaning of simple text features.	I can identify the features of an explanation text.

Unit 2 Explanations

Learning outcomes	Assessment opportunity and evidence	Assessment focuses (AFs) Level 1	Success criteria
Making a pictorial flow chart Children can make choices about the best way to present information in an explanation text using flow charts and diagrams.	• Paired activity where children create their own pictorial flow chart to show the life cycle of a pea. • Teacher observation and partner discussion. • Children's completed pictorial flow charts.	**Reading AF4** Some awareness of meaning of simple text features.	• I can identify the features of an explanation text. • I can identify ways of presenting an explanation. • I can create a pictorial flow chart.
Phase ④ activity page 92			
Using a cyclical flow chart Children note information collected in another curriculum area and the use of visual representation that models a process. This is presented as a written and diagrammatic explanation text.	• Paired activity where children discuss the purpose and advantages of using a cyclical flow chart and create their own cyclical flow charts to show the life cycle of a pea. • Partner conversation. • Children's completed cyclical flow charts.	**Writing AF3** • Some formulaic phrases indicate start/end of text. • Events/ideas sometimes in appropriate order.	• I can recognise and make a cyclical flow chart. • I can write an explanation text. • I can present and evaluate explanations.

Learning outcomes	Assessment opportunity and evidence	Assessment focuses (AFs)		Success criteria
		Level 2	Level 3	
Phase ① activities pages 87–88				
Identifying key words Children can find a key word using an index and then locate the relevant information on a page.	• Independent or paired activity where children identify key words relating to a topic and then use an index to identify where they would go to find out more information. • Children's completed photocopiables.	**Reading AF2** • Some specific straightforward information recalled. • Generally clear idea of where to look for information.	**Reading AF2** • Simple, most obvious points identified though there may also be some misunderstanding. • Some comments include quotations from or references to text, but not always relevant.	• I can identify key words. • I can use an index to find information in a book.
Creating order Children can make and use a glossary of special interest words related to an investigation.	• Group activity where children play a game, putting key words into alphabetical order and then type up their own index. • Children's completed indexes.	**Writing AF2** • Some basic purpose established. • Some appropriate features of the given form used. • Some attempts to adopt appropriate style.	**Writing AF2** • Purpose established at a general level. • Main features of selected form sometimes signalled to the reader. • Some attempts at appropriate style, with attention to reader.	• I can put words in alphabetical order. • I can make a glossary.
Phase ② activities pages 89–90				
Modelling and explaining Children can model a process using models, pictures and diagrams and explain the process to peers.	• Paired and group activity where children create and present a human flow chart to model the life cycle of a pea. • Partner discussion. • Children's completed peer assessments.	**Reading AF4** Some awareness of use of features of organisation.	**Reading AF4** A few basic features of organisation at text level identified, with little or no linked comment.	• I can explain a process to others using models, pictures and diagrams. • I can present and evaluate explanations.

Unit 2 ▢ Explanations

Learning outcomes	Assessment opportunity and evidence	Assessment focuses (AFs)		Success criteria
		Level 2	Level 3	
Presenting and evaluating Children can model a process using models, pictures and diagrams and explain the process to peers.	• Paired activity where children rehearse and give a presentation of their individual pictorial flow chart and assess their own presentation using the photocopiable. • Paired rehearsal and individual oral presentations. • Children's completed self-assessment.	**Writing AF7** • Simple, often speech-like vocabulary conveys relevant meanings. • Some adventurous word choices.	**Writing AF7** • Simple, generally appropriate vocabulary used, limited in range. • Some words selected for effect or occasion.	• I can identify ways of presenting an explanation. • I can present and evaluate explanations.

Phase ③ activities pages 90–91

Identifying explanation features Children can recognise the structure and language features of an explanation text.	• Paired activity where children complete an interactive activity, spotting key features of an explanation text and complete the differentiated photocopiable to reinforce what they have learned. • Partner discussion and completion of the interactive activity. • Children's completed photocopiables.	**Reading AF4** Some awareness of use of features of organisation.	**Reading AF4** A few basic features of organisation at text level identified, with little or no linked comment.	I can identify the features of an explanation text.
Making a pictorial flow chart Children can make choices about the best way to present information in an explanation text using flow charts and diagrams.	• Paired and independent activity where children create their own pictorial flow chart to show the life cycle of a pea. • Teacher observation and partner discussion. • Children's completed pictorial flow charts.	**Reading AF4** Some awareness of use of features of organisation.	**Reading AF4** A few basic features of organisation at text level identified, with little or no linked comment.	• I can identify the features of an explanation text. • I can identify ways of presenting an explanation. • I can create a pictorial flow chart.

Phase ④ activity page 92

Using a cyclical flow chart Children note information collected in another curriculum area and the use of visual representation that models a process. This is presented as a written and diagrammatic explanation text.	• Independent and paired activity where children discuss the purpose and advantages of using a cyclical flow chart and create their own cyclical flow charts to show the life cycle of a pea. • Partner conversation. • Children's completed cyclical flow charts.	**Writing AF3** • Some basic sequencing of ideas or material. • Openings and/or closings sometimes signalled.	**Writing AF3** • Some attempt to organise ideas with related points placed next to each other. • Openings and closings usually signalled. • Some attempt to sequence ideas or material logically.	• I can recognise and make a cyclical flow chart. • I can write an explanation text. • I can present and evaluate explanations.

Phase ① Identifying key words

Learning outcome
Children can find a key word using an index and then locate the relevant information on a page.

Success criteria
- I can identify key words.
- I can use an index to find information in a book.

Setting the context
Before beginning this assessment, ensure the children have already completed a classroom science investigation. For example, growing plants from seeds. Remind the children of this previous work.

Assessment opportunity
Ask the children to write one key word related to this previous work on their individual whiteboards. Invite them to hold these up. Put the children into pairs of similar ability to compare and justify their choices. Next, suggest that the children prepare, independently or with their partner, a list of key words to help another child do this same science work next year. Ask them to list about eight key words related to the work. Afterwards, use the photocopiable page 'Key words' to copy a sample list onto the whiteboard. Give the children the photocopiable page 'Using key words' to list their own words and some of those from your sample list. Then, give out the photocopiable page 'Index', explaining it is the index from the back of a book on plants. Ask them to identify and write on their photocopiable worksheet ('Using key words') the page number that they would go to in order to find information relating to their key word.

Assessment evidence
At level 1, the children will list some key words, but may rely heavily on your list. Working with a partner, they will identify some pages correctly. At levels 2–3, the children will write more of their own key words and will identify a relevant page for most of these. They may sometimes consult a partner. This activity will provide evidence towards Reading AF2.

Next steps
Support: If the children struggle to think of key words, suggest they look at their science work on the topic.
Extension: Suggest the children make a list of ten key words relating to their current science work. Challenge them to use the index of a non-fiction book to identify a useful page for each word.

Key aspects of learning
Enquiry: Children will carry out their own enquiry or investigation in another area of the curriculum, and will make observations and explain what they have found out. Throughout their enquiry, children will be encouraged to pose questions prior to, during and after their investigation. They will decide the most appropriate presentation for their findings.
Information processing: Children will identify relevant information from observation and practical experience, information texts and ICT texts and select this to help them write their own explanation text for an individual or class book or wall display.

Phase ① Creating order

Learning outcome
Children can make and use a glossary of special interest words related to an investigation.

Success criteria
● I can put words in alphabetical order.
● I can make a glossary.

Setting the context
The children should have already completed the previous activity and be familiar with using the index and glossary of a non-fiction book. Enlarge and print several copies of the photocopiable page 'Key words'. Cut out the words and keep these to hand, ready for the game introduced later on in this assessment.

Assessment opportunity
Perform this assessment in small groups, so that you can readily observe the children's individual contributions. Display the photocopiable page 'Index'. Ask the children to think about the order in which the words are listed and to work out the reason for that order. Invite them to tell a partner or write their answer on their individual whiteboard. Listen and watch for recognition of alphabetical order. Next, put the children into groups of three. Give each child one of the cut-out words and then challenge them, in their groups, to arrange themselves into alphabetical order. (Designate one side of the room as the beginning of their line.) After each successful turn, change one or two of the group's words for the group to re-order itself. Afterwards, give the children a copy of the photocopiable page 'Key words' for the children to type and create an on-screen index. Ask the children working at levels 2–3 to identify eight words they think need definitions to create an easy-to-use glossary.

Assessment evidence
At level 1, the children may need to play the game in pairs, with the list of key words reduced for when they type their index. At levels 2–3, the children will play the game with considerable success, make only a few mistakes when typing their index and be able to create a glossary with acceptable definitions. This activity will provide evidence towards Writing AF2.

Next steps
Support: If the children struggle with the game, give adult support, playing the game as an on-screen activity, before the children play in pairs.
Extension: Challenge the children to add eight more words of their own, relevant to a book on plants, and add them, including definitions, to their glossary.

Key aspects of learning
Enquiry: Children will carry out their own enquiry or investigation in another area of the curriculum, and will make observations and explain what they have found out. Throughout their enquiry, children will be encouraged to pose questions prior to, during and after their investigation. They will decide the most appropriate presentation for their findings.

Phase ② Modelling and explaining

Learning outcome
Children can model a process using models, pictures and diagrams and explain the process to peers.

Success criteria
● I can explain a process to others using models, pictures and diagrams.
● I can present and evaluate explanations.

Setting the context
The children will need to have read explanation texts and they should have some awareness of the key features of this text type. Provide the class with copies of the photocopiable page 'How do peas grow?'. Read through the text together and briefly discuss some of the features of an explanation text.

Assessment opportunity
In pairs, ask the children to re-read the text and identify the stages of the pea's growth. Expand the pairs into discussion groups of four to six children of comparable ability. Suggest the groups allocate a stage in the pea's process to each group member – that person is then responsible for drawing a quick sketch on a sheet of paper to represent that stage. After the drawings are complete, ask groups to arrange themselves into a human flow chart, to show the correct sequence of stages. Each child, in turn, should hold up their sheet of paper and explain their stage of the process. Watch and listen to the group flow charts. The children in the audience can complete the photocopiable page 'Watching an explanation' to record their views on each presentation.

Assessment evidence
At level 1, children should have some ideas to contribute to the group discussion and will identify some stages in the pea process. They may lack the confidence to work independently in the group presentation, instead needing the support of a partner for their stage in the human flow chart. At levels 2–3, children will identify clear stages in the pea's development and make a contribution to the human flow chart. This activity will provide evidence towards Reading AF4.

Next steps
Support: If the children struggle with taking an independent role in the flow chart, put them with a partner.
Extension: Suggest the children complete an assessment of their own group's presentation, using the photocopiable page 'Watching an explanation'.

Key aspects of learning
Evaluation: Children will present information orally and in writing, in the form of a flow chart or cyclic diagram. They will be able to support their judgements with their own evidence, drawing on a range of sources to support their evaluation.
Communication: Children will develop their ability to express and communicate in spoken, pictorial and written form a simple explanation of a process. They may also communicate their ideas using a variety of prompts, including models, diagrams and charts.

Unit 2 🔲 **Explanations**

Phase ② Presenting and evaluating

Learning outcome
Children can model a process using models, pictures and diagrams and explain the process to peers.

Success criteria
- I can identify ways of presenting an explanation.
- I can present and evaluate explanations.

Setting the context
Remind the children of their group pictorial flow charts (see page 89). Return these flow charts to the children for reference. Suggest that the flow charts would now benefit from an oral explanation to make their meaning clear.

Assessment opportunity
Put the children into pairs to rehearse their presentation. Remind them to think about their language and gestures as they explain their flow chart. When the children finally present their pictorial flow chart to a group, let them add realism by using a scanner and an interactive whiteboard. Afterwards, give the children the self-assessment photocopiable page 'Three stars and a wish' to complete.

Assessment evidence
At level 1, the children will prefer to present their presentation with a partner, but should be able to make an individual contribution. They should use some appropriate language and gestures. Their self-assessment will be brief but should show some understanding of what they have done. At levels 2–3, the children will be able to present their flow chart with helpful gestures and language. Their self-assessment should show a level of self-perception. This activity will provide evidence towards Writing AF7.

Next steps
Support: If the children lack self-confidence, let them make their final presentation to an audience of only one or two.
Extension: Suggest the children make a peer assessment of their partner's presentation, using the photocopiable page 'Three stars and a wish', discussing their comments with them afterwards.

Key aspects of learning
Evaluation: Children will present information orally and in writing, in the form of a flow chart or cyclic diagram. They will be able to support their judgements with their own evidence, drawing on a range of sources to support their evaluation.
Communication: Children will develop their ability to express and communicate in spoken, pictorial and written form a simple explanation of a process. They may also communicate their ideas using a variety of prompts, including models, diagrams and charts.

Phase ③ Identifying explanation features

Learning outcome
Children can recognise the structure and language features of an explanation text.

Success criteria
I can identify the features of an explanation text.

Setting the context
Ensure the children have read explanations and discussed organisational and language features. Explain that they are going to view extracts from an explanation text.

Assessment opportunity
Put the children into pairs to do the interactive activity 'Finding features'. Encourage

them to discuss each question and decide a likely answer before they find and click on the hot spot to check. Suggest the children repeat the activity so they can assess their improvement. Afterwards, give them a copy of the photocopiable page 'How do peas grow?' to read and to help them complete the photocopiable page 'Features of an explanation text' (version 1 or 2).

Assessment evidence
At level 1, the children may find the interactive activity difficult, but their performance should improve when repeating the exercise. With some reading support, they should complete most of the photocopiable page correctly. At levels 2–3, the children will have a lively discussion about the interactive questions and will predict many correct answers. They will identify many of the features when reading 'How do peas grow?' and will cope independently with the photocopiable page. This activity will provide evidence towards Reading AF4.

Next steps
Support: If the children struggle with the interactive activity, give adult support, reading aloud the question and prompting them for answers.
Extension: Suggest the children annotate 'How do peas grow?' so that they can write notes identifying and commenting on features.

Key aspects of learning
Communication: Children will develop their ability to express and communicate in spoken, pictorial and written form a simple explanation of a process. They may also communicate their ideas using a variety of prompts, including models, diagrams and charts.

Phase ③ Making a pictorial flow chart

Learning outcome
Children can make choices about the best way to present information in an explanation text using flow charts and diagrams.

Success criteria
- I can identify the features of an explanation text.
- I can identify ways of presenting an explanation.
- I can create a pictorial flow chart.

Setting the context
Prior to this assessment, the children should have read explanation texts featuring diagrams. They will also need to have created a group pictorial flow chart showing the stages in the life cycle of a pea. Enlarge and display the photocopiable page 'How do peas grow?' for everyone to re-read. Ask the children to write on their individual whiteboards and hold up the name of the helpful feature that is missing from this explanation text. (A flow chart/diagram.)

Assessment opportunity
Put the children into pairs to discuss their flow chart and how it could have been improved. Leave the children working at level 1 in pairs, but let those working at levels 2–3 work independently from this point. Display the photocopiable page 'A pictorial flow chart', explaining that you want the children to reconstruct their own flow chart in pictorial form. Suggest planning and doing rough drafts before they do their final pictures for each stage on the photocopiable page. Save the completed charts to use in the next activity.

Assessment evidence
At level 1, the children may need to revise forming a group human flow chart before doing this new task. They will benefit from partner discussion and adult support as they do initial pictorial drafts. At levels 2–3, the children will discuss their previous human flow chart and have improvement ideas. They should be able to do their final work independently. This activity will provide evidence towards Reading AF4.

Unit 2 ⬜ **Explanations**

▷ **Next steps**
Support: Suggest the children talk through each stage with a partner.
Extension: Suggest the children use a non-fiction book related to design and technology and find an explanation text. Can they identify a number of stages in the process? Can they work out what a pictorial flow chart would look like?

Key aspects of learning
Evaluation: Children will present information orally and in writing, in the form of a flow chart or cyclic diagram. They will be able to support their judgements with their own evidence, drawing on a range of sources to support their evaluation.
Communication: Children will develop their ability to express and communicate in spoken, pictorial and written form a simple explanation of a process. They may also communicate their ideas using a variety of prompts, including models, diagrams and charts.

Phase ④ Using a cyclical flow chart

Learning outcome
Children note information collected in another curriculum area and the use of visual representation that models a process. This is presented as a written and diagrammatic explanation text.

Success criteria
● I can recognise and make a cyclical flow chart.
● I can write an explanation text.
● I can present and evaluate explanations.

Setting the context
Ensure the children have had experience of seeing explanations presented in the form of a cyclical flow chart and have identified their suitability for particular explanations. They should also have created a human flow chart and a pictorial flow chart (see Phase 2 and Phase 3 activities). They will also need to have learned about plant life cycles in science topic work.

Assessment opportunity
Put the children into pairs of comparable ability. Display a copy of the photocopiable page 'A cyclical flow chart'. Invite the children to share their opinions of this type of diagram with their partner. Listen as partners share answers in response to your questions. For example, *What happens in this type of diagram?* Next, ask the children to remind each other of the life cycle of a pea. Give them each a copy of the photocopiable page 'A cyclical flow chart' and suggest that they plan and then draw pictures in the empty circles to show the most important stages of the pea's growth. Afterwards, ask them to write a sentence next to each picture saying what happens at that stage.

Assessment evidence
At level 1, the children will need reminding of the purpose of a cyclical flow chart. They may need help with ordering their pictures and sentences. Their writing may be limited to phrases or oral explanations. At levels 2–3, the children will know the importance of this diagram's format. They will attempt to organise the pictures and writing on the cyclical flow chart in a logical sequence. This activity will provide evidence towards Writing AF3.

Next steps
Support: Return to their previous pictorial flow chart from the Phase 3 activity 'Making a pictorial flow chart' to help them decide on stages and pictures.
Extension: Suggest the children make a cyclical flow chart of a sunflower's growth.

Key aspects of learning
Evaluation: Children will present information orally and in writing, in the form of a flow chart or cyclic diagram. They will be able to support their judgements with their own evidence, drawing on a range of sources to support their evaluation.

Periodic assessment

Reading

Learning outcomes
- Children demonstrate that they have understood information read from a book or screen by noting the main points.
- Children can make choices about the best way to present information in an explanation text, using flow charts and diagrams.

Success criteria
- I can find information in a text.
- I can add a flow chart or diagram to a text.

Setting the context
Prior to this assessment, ensure the children have had experience of reading explanation texts and seeing a variety of accompanying diagrams. They should recognise why some are more appropriate than others.

Assessment opportunity
Put the children into pairs of comparable ability and give them the photocopiable page 'Non-fiction 2 Reading assessment text' to read together. Assess their reading comprehension as they read and discuss the text with a partner. Let the children progress to the interactive activity 'Non-fiction 2 Reading assessment (a)'. Observe how they reference the text and make use of key words to answer the questions. Afterwards, give children the photocopiable page 'Non-fiction 2 Reading assessment (b)' to complete independently. At level 1, support the children in reading the text, both on screen and on the photocopiable page. Afterwards, suggest that the explanation text would be improved by a diagram. Listen as partners discuss ideas. Ask the children to list possible formats, choosing and creating their own diagram. Let those working at level 1 work with a partner.

Assessment evidence
At level 1, the children will need support when reading, and will use a considerable amount of trial and error to complete the interactive activity. They should have some correct answers on the photocopiable page and will produce a diagram of some relevance. At levels 2–3, the children will read the text with minimal support. When doing the interactive activity, they will use the text well, locating information with the help of key words. They will be certain in their selection of many answers. They will list more than one possible format for a diagram and create a diagram that adds to the clarity of the explanation. This activity will help you judge the children's overall understanding of work in this unit and provide evidence against Reading AF1, AF2, AF4 and AF6.

Periodic assessment

NON-FICTION

Writing

Learning outcomes
● Children can note information collected from more than one source.
● Children can construct a pictorial flow chart.
● Children can write and evaluate explanation texts.

Success criteria
● I can make a pictorial flow chart.
● I can write an explanation text.
● I can present and evaluate explanations.

Setting the context
Ensure the children have already completed the Phase 4 activity, 'Planning an explanation'. Return the pictorial flow charts to the children, reminding them of the work they did in Phase 4 and the objectives of their flow chart.

Assessment opportunity
Put the children into pairs to discuss their original practical work, comparing it with the pictorial flow chart that they produced. Let them use their flow chart as a plan, writing notes on it of any additional information they think it needs to help improve it. Suggest that on the back of their diagram, they make a checklist of important writing features for their explanation text. Provide a possible *How* or *Why* title and write it on the whiteboard. Then invite the children to begin writing their explanation text, using the flow chart and the checklist as a guide. Observe the children's ability to write, edit, make changes to and improve their text. (Writing on screen would make this easier.) Allow time for them to decide on a format for a diagram and create it. Afterwards, ask them to think about how they will present their explanation. Give each child a copy of the photocopiable page 'Non-fiction 2 Writing assessment'. Put the children into pairs for each child to make a presentation to their partner, who can then evaluate the written, visual and verbal explanation using the photocopiable page.

Assessment evidence
At level 1, the children will need prompting to remember the original practical work and their pictorial flow chart. Their notes will be few and their checklist usually written in response to leading questions. They should write an explanation that shows links to their pictorial flow chart, but their new diagram may be the same. They should be able to make a simple partner evaluation. At levels 2–3, the children will remember previous work and be able to make some written notes and a useful checklist. They will write a longer text, making good use of their pictorial plan, checklist and editing skills. Their choice of diagram should improve the clarity of their text. Their partner evaluation will often demonstrate perception and observation. This activity will help you judge the children's overall understanding of work in this unit and provide evidence against Writing AF2, AF3 and AF7.

How do peas grow?

A pea is a seed for a new pea plant. First the seed is planted in soil. The seed then grows roots. As the roots grow downwards, they hold the seed in place. The seed grows a shoot. Because the shoot grows upwards, it pushes above the soil.

The shoot grows into a plant with flowers. The flowers make pea pods. Inside the pea pods are new peas. When the pods split open, the peas fall out.

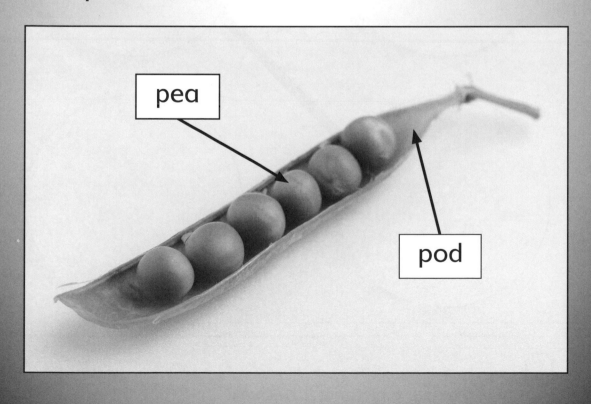

Photograph © Photos.com / GettyImages.

NON-FICTION

Name _____   Date _____

A pictorial flow chart

How _____ ?

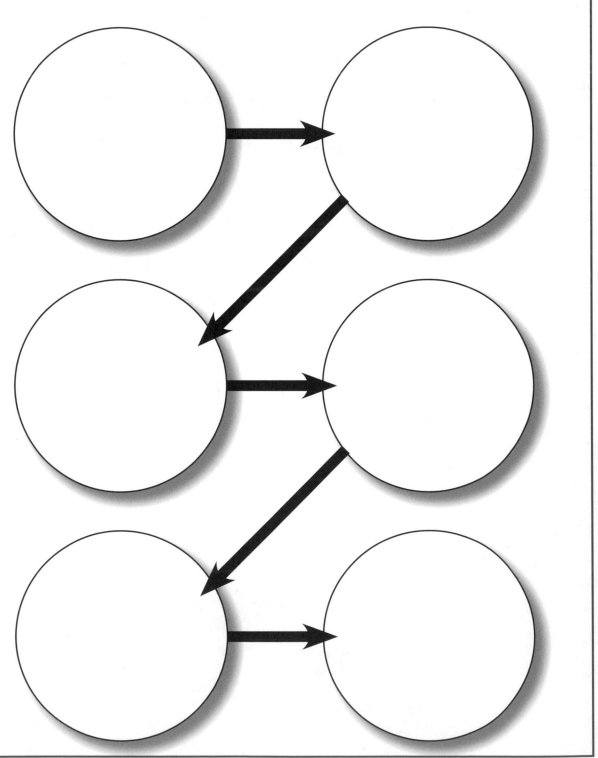

Red Amber Green

I can create a pictorial flow chart. ☐

Non-fiction 2 Reading assessment text

How does a frog develop?

A frog can live on land and in water. An adult frog lays its eggs in water. The eggs are inside a jelly material called frogspawn.

When an egg hatches, a small tadpole with a long tail comes out of the egg and the frogspawn. As it gets bigger, the tadpole grows legs. Then, its long tail shrinks and the tadpole becomes a young frog. After the young frog has grown more, it is an adult, so it can lay new eggs.

Photograph © Photo.com /JupiterImages.

NON-FICTION

UNIT 3 Information texts

Literacy objectives

Speak and listen for a wide range of purposes in different contexts

Strand 1 Speaking
- Explain ideas and processes using imaginative and adventurous vocabulary and non-verbal gestures to support communication.

Strand 2 Listening and responding
- Listen to others in class, ask relevant questions and follow instructions.

Strand 3 Group discussion and interaction
- Listen to each other's views and preferences, agree the next steps to take and identify contributions by each group member.

Read and write for a range of purposes on paper and on screen

Strand 5 Word recognition: decoding (reading) and encoding (spelling)
- Read independently and with increasing fluency longer and less familiar texts.
- Spell with increasing accuracy and confidence, drawing on word recognition and knowledge of word structure, and spelling patterns.
- Know how to tackle unfamiliar words that are not completely decodable.
- Read and spell less common alternative graphemes including trigraphs.
- Read high and medium frequency words independently and automatically.

Strand 6 Word structure and spelling
- Spell with increasing accuracy and confidence, drawing on word recognition and knowledge of word structure, and spelling patterns including common inflections and use of double letters.
- Read and spell less common alternative graphemes including trigraphs.

Strand 7 Understanding and interpreting texts
- Draw together ideas and information from across a whole text, using simple signposts in the text.
- Explain organisational features of texts, including alphabetical order, layout, diagrams, captions, hyperlinks and bullet points.
- Explore how particular words are used, including words and expressions with similar meanings.

Strand 8 Engaging with and responding to texts
- Explain their reactions to texts, commenting on important aspects.

Strand 9 Creating and shaping texts
- Draw on knowledge and experience of texts in deciding and planning what and how to write.
- Make adventurous word and language choices appropriate to the style and purpose of the text.
- Select from different presentational features to suit particular writing purposes.

Strand 10 Text structure and organisation
- Use planning to establish clear sections for writing.
- Use appropriate language to make sections hang together.

Strand 11 Sentence structure and punctuation
- Write simple and compound sentences and begin to use subordination in relation to time and reason.
- Compose sentences using tense consistently (present and past).
- Use question marks, and use commas to separate items in a list.

Strand 12 Presentation
- Word-process short narrative and non-narrative texts.

Key aspects of learning

Enquiry
● Children will ask questions arising from work in another area of the curriculum, research and then plan how to present the information effectively.

Information processing
● Children will identify relevant information from a range of sources on paper and on screen and use this to write their own information texts.

Communication
● Children will develop their ability to discuss as they work collaboratively in paired, group and whole-class contexts. They will develop their ability to listen critically to broadcast information and to make an oral presentation. They will also communicate outcomes in writing.

Assessment focuses

Reading
AF1 *(use a range of strategies, including accurate decoding of text, to read for meaning).*
AF2 *(understand, describe, select or retrieve information, events or ideas from texts and use quotation and reference to text).*

Writing
AF1 *(write imaginative, interesting and thoughtful texts).*
AF2 *(produce texts which are appropriate to task, reader and purpose).*

Speaking and listening
Speaking (speak in an organised manner; use detail).
Listening and responding (respond to presentations by repeating some highlights and commenting constructively).
Group discussion and interaction (contribute to group, allocate tasks, consider alternatives and reach agreement).

Resources

Phase 1 activities
Interactive activity, 'Florence Nightingale'
Photocopiable page, 'Finding answers about Samuel Pepys'
Phase 2 activities
Photocopiable page, 'Questions about Samuel Pepys'
Photocopiable page, 'The Story of Samuel Pepys' (versions 1 and 2)
Phase 3 activities
Photocopiable page, 'The Story of Samuel Pepys' (versions 1 and 2)
Photocopiable page, 'Comparing sources of information'
Periodic assessment
Photocopiable page, 'Non-fiction 3 Reading assessment'
Photocopiable page, 'Non-fiction 3 Reading assessment text'
Photocopiable page, 'Non-fiction 3 Writing assessment'

Unit 3 Information texts

Learning outcomes	Assessment opportunity and evidence	Assessment focuses (AFs)	Success criteria
		Level 1	
Phase ① activities pages 103–104			
Asking questions Children can pose questions for investigation and understand the layout of information in a factual book.	• Paired activity where children perform an interactive activity to match questions to chapter headings and write their own list of questions to find out about Samuel Pepys. • Children's discussions, completed interactive activities and written questions.	**Reading AF2** • Some simple points from familiar texts recalled. • Some pages/sections of interest located.	• I can ask questions. • I know where to start looking for information in a book.
Finding answers Children can find answers to questions quickly using the information in a factual book.	• Paired activity where children discuss the sections of an information book, how they would use them and complete an unfinished contents page. • Children's discussion and written work.	**Writing AF2** Some indication of basic purpose, particular form or awareness of reader.	• I can ask questions. • I know where to start looking for information in a book.
Phase ② activities pages 105–106			
Reading and noting Children can make simple notes from books and ICT texts.	• Paired activity where children are provided with an information text about Samuel Pepys and use it to find answers to their questions, recording these as notes on the photocopiable. • Children's discussions and written notes.	**Reading AF1** • Some high frequency and familiar words read fluently and automatically. • Decode familiar and some unfamiliar words using blending as the prime approach. • Some awareness of punctuation marks.	• I can find information in a non-fiction text. • I can make notes from a non-fiction text.
Using a website Children can make simple notes from books and ICT texts.	• Paired activity where children use a website to find out about Samuel Pepys to find answers to their questions and record them as notes on the photocopiable. • Partner discussion and use of the website to find information. • Children's written notes on the photocopiable.	**Reading AF2** • Some simple points from familiar texts recalled. • Some pages/sections of interest located.	• I can find information on a website. • I can make notes from an ICT text.

Unit 3 📖 Information texts

Learning outcomes	Assessment opportunity and evidence	Assessment focuses (AFs)	Success criteria
		Level 1	

Phase ③ activities pages 106–107

Learning outcomes	Assessment opportunity and evidence	Assessment focuses (AFs) — Level 1	Success criteria
Evaluating resources Children can compare and evaluate research material from books and ICT texts.	● Paired activity where children discuss and then produce a comparison of printed information ICT versions of text. ● Children's discussions and written evaluations.	**Reading AF2** ● Some simple points from familiar texts recalled. ● Some pages/sections of interest located.	● I can find information in a non-fiction text. ● I can compare ICT texts and books and evaluate how useful they are.
Planning research Children can pose and record questions for investigation.	● Paired activity where children devise a list of questions to help find out more about Edward Jenner. ● Children's discussions and written questions.	**Writing AF1** ● Basic information and ideas conveyed through appropriate word choice. ● Some descriptive language.	● I can ask questions. ● I can write questions. ● I can compare ICT texts and books and evaluate how useful they are.

Learning outcomes	Assessment opportunity and evidence	Assessment focuses (AFs)		Success criteria
		Level 2	Level 3	

Phase ① activities pages 103–104

Learning outcomes	Assessment opportunity and evidence	Assessment focuses (AFs) — Level 2	Assessment focuses (AFs) — Level 3	Success criteria
Asking questions Children can pose questions for investigation and understand the layout of information in a factual book.	● Paired activity where children perform an interactive activity to match questions to chapter headings and write their own list of questions to find out about Samuel Pepys. ● Partner discussion and completion of the interactive activity. ● Children's written questions.	**Reading AF2** ● Some specific straightforward information recalled. ● Generally clear idea of where to look for information.	**Reading AF2** ● Simple, most obvious points identified though there may also be some misunderstanding. ● Some comments include quotations from or references to text, but not always relevant.	● I can ask questions. ● I know where to start looking for information in a book.
Finding answers Children can find answers to questions quickly using the information in a factual book.	● Paired activity where children discuss the sections of an information book, how they would use them and complete an unfinished contents page. ● Partner discussion, showing understanding of the format of an information book. ● Children's written work on the photocopiable.	**Writing AF2** ● Some basic purpose established. ● Some appropriate features of the given form used. ● Some attempts to adopt appropriate style.	**Writing AF2** ● Purpose established at a general level. ● Main features of selected form sometimes signalled to the reader. ● Some attempts at appropriate style, with attention to reader.	● I can ask questions. ● I know where to start looking for information in a book.

Unit 3 🔲 Information texts

Learning outcomes	Assessment opportunity and evidence	Assessment focuses (AFs)		Success criteria
		Level 2	Level 3	
Phase ② activities pages 105–106				
Reading and noting Children can make simple notes from books and ICT texts.	• Paired activity where children are provided with text about Samuel Pepys and use it to find answers to their questions, recording these as notes on the photocopiable. • Partner discussion and use of the text to find information. • Children's written notes on the photocopiable.	**Reading AF1** • Range of key words read on sight. • Unfamiliar words decoded using appropriate strategies. • Some fluency and expression.	**Reading AF1** Range of strategies used mostly effectively to read with fluency, understanding and expression.	• I can find information in a non-fiction text. • I can make notes from a non-fiction text.
Using a website Children can make simple notes from books and ICT texts.	• Paired activity where children use a website about Samuel Pepys to find answers to their questions and record them as notes on the photocopiable. • Partner discussion and use of the website to find information. • Children's written notes on the photocopiable.	**Reading AF2** • Some specific, straightforward information recalled. • Generally clear idea of where to look for information.	**Reading AF2** • Simple, most obvious points identified though there may also be some misunderstanding. • Some comments include quotations from or references to text, but not always relevant..	• I can find information on a website. • I can make notes from an ICT text.
Phase ③ activities pages 106–107				
Evaluating resources Children can compare and evaluate research material from books and ICT texts.	• Paired activity where children discuss and then produce a comparison of printed and ICT versions of information text. • Partner discussion. • Children's written evaluations on the photocopiable.	**Reading AF2** • Some specific, straightforward information recalled. • Generally clear idea of where to look for information.	**Reading AF2** • Simple, most obvious points identified though there may also be some misunderstanding. • Some comments include quotations from or references to text, but not always relevant	• I can find information in a non-fiction text. • I can compare ICT texts and books and evaluate how useful they are.
Planning research Children can pose and record questions for investigation.	• Independent and paired activity where children are given a new history topic on Edward Jenner and devise a list of questions to help find out more about him. • Partner discussion of useful *wh-* words and information texts. • Children's independently written questions.	**Writing AF1** • Mostly relevant ideas and content, sometimes repetitive or sparse. • Some apt word choices create interest. • Brief comments, questions about events or actions suggest viewpoint.	**Writing AF1** • Some appropriate ideas and content included. • Some attempt to elaborate on basic information or events. • Attempt to adopt viewpoint, though often not maintained or inconsistent.	• I can ask questions. • I can write questions. • I can compare ICT texts and books and evaluate how useful they are.

Phase ① Asking questions

Learning outcome
Children can pose questions for investigation and understand the layout of information in a factual book.

Success criteria
● I can ask questions.
● I know where to start looking for information in a book.

Setting the context
Prior to this assessment, the children should have used non-fiction to look for information and to answer their own questions about a topic. Begin the session by asking the children to imagine that they are starting a new history topic on Florence Nightingale. They have been given a book about Florence Nightingale and have been challenged to find the answers to four questions.

Assessment opportunity
Give the children the interactive activity 'Florence Nightingale'. In pairs, ask them to decide which chapter would best suit each question. Listen as they discuss and select their answers, noticing the degree of trial and error involved. Afterwards, ask the children to imagine they are now doing a history topic on Samuel Pepys. In their pairs, invite them to think about the six likely questions that they would ask about Pepys. Then, give each child a sheet of paper to record their questions.

Assessment evidence
At level 1, the children may need support reading the interactive activity and will match questions to chapters with considerable trial and error. Their lists may only have three or four simple questions. At levels 2–3, the children will be quicker to recognise links between the information being asked for and the chapter headings provided. Partners should discuss ideas, demonstrate reasoning and use less trial and error. Their lists of questions will demonstrate more depth. This activity will provide evidence towards Reading AF2.

Next steps
Support: If the children struggle to think of questions, suggest they first do role play, someone (perhaps an adult) taking the role of Pepys, while the children ask a question orally.
Extension: Suggest children compare lists with a partner, discussing which questions are likely to gain the most information about Pepys.

Key aspects of learning
Enquiry: Children will ask questions arising from work in another area of the curriculum, research and then plan how to present the information effectively.
Communication: Children will develop their ability to discuss as they work collaboratively in paired, group and whole-class contexts. They will develop their ability to listen critically to broadcast information and to make an oral presentation. They will also communicate outcomes in writing.

NON-FICTION

Phase ① Finding answers

Learning outcome
Children can find answers to questions quickly using the information in a factual book.

Success criteria
- I can ask questions.
- I know where to start looking for information in a book.

Setting the context
Ensure the children have had prior experience of searching for information in non-fiction books to answer specific questions. They should have also completed the previous activity. Begin by reminding the children of this previous work, and returning their lists of questions about Samuel Pepys.

Assessment opportunity
Ask the children to imagine that they have been given a book called 'Samuel Pepys'. How would they go about finding the answers to the questions on their sheet? Let them write on their individual whiteboard a place in the book they would choose to start. Watch for their knowledge of correct, relevant terms such as 'contents' and 'index', and their location in the book. In pairs, provide each child with a copy of the photocopiable 'Finding answers about Samuel Pepys'. Explain that it shows the unfinished contents page of the book about Samuel Pepys. Ask the children to re-read their questions carefully and then complete the contents page, writing chapter titles to suit their questions. Let them cut out their questions and stick them on the left-hand side of the photocopiable page, next to the chapter title they think will answer their question. (If space does not allow this, let children draw 'match-up' lines between a question and a chapter.)

Assessment evidence
At level 1, the children may not remember the terms 'contents' and 'index' but should be able to describe one of them, perhaps in different language. Their chapter headings may be similar to their questions. At levels 2–3, the children will remember at least one correct term and describe how they would use it to search for information. Their chapter titles will be interesting and demonstrate greater breadth. This activity will provide evidence towards Writing AF2.

Next steps
Support: If children struggle with the photocopiable page, suggest they work with a partner and a combined selection of their questions.
Extension: Remind the children that there is usually a page number for each chapter. Ask them to fill in the missing page numbers.

Key aspects of learning
Enquiry: Children will ask questions arising from work in another area of the curriculum, research and then plan how to present the information effectively.
Information processing: Children will identify relevant information from a range of sources on paper and on screen and use this to write their own information texts.

Phase ② Reading and noting

Success criteria
● I can find information in a non-fiction text.
● I can make notes from a non-fiction text.

Setting the context
Ensure the children have experience of reading non-fiction information texts and have searched non-fiction books for information they need to answer specific questions. They should already have completed the first activity in this unit.

Assessment opportunity
Give children the photocopiable page 'Questions about Samuel Pepys'. Explain that it is a list of questions that you would like to have answered about Samuel Pepys. Display and read aloud the photocopiable page 'The Story of Samuel Pepys' (version 1 or 2). Afterwards, put children into pairs with a copy of the text (version 1 or 2). Suggest partners re-read the text, and then work through the questions looking for answers. Remind them that their answers only need to be written in note form (not complete sentences), but names and dates should be copied accurately.

Assessment evidence
At level 1, the children will need additional reading support, but should be able to identify some answers. They will often copy text rather than write notes. At levels 2–3, the children should cope without adult support, and will search the text more systematically for answers. They should be helped by an awareness of key words and organisational devices. They may need to be reminded that notes are not the same as sentences. This activity will provide evidence towards Reading AF1.

Next steps
Support: If the children struggle to find an answer, reduce their search by directing them to the relevant section of the text.
Extension: Ask the children to provide an appropriate illustration or diagram to accompany the text.

Key aspects of learning
Information processing: Children will identify relevant information from a range of sources on paper and on screen and use this to write their own information texts.

Phase ② Using a website

Success criteria
● I can find information on a website.
● I can make notes from an ICT text.

Setting the context
Ensure the children have had experience of investigating websites and searching non-fiction texts to find answers to specific questions. They should also have completed the previous activity.

Assessment opportunity
Put children into pairs, with a computer that has internet access. Remind them of the previous activity and their search of a printed text for answers about Samuel Pepys. Suggest that they now try answering the same questions by using information on screen. Give the children a fresh copy of the photocopiable page 'Questions about Samuel Pepys' and direct them to a relevant website. For example,

NON-FICTION

▷ www.bbc.co.uk/schools/famouspeople/standard/pepys/learn Discuss some features of the site, such as hot spots, the help button and glossary, but also allow partners to work together and explore the site for themselves. Remind them to write notes on their photocopiable pages to answer the questions provided. Observe their ability to navigate the website, extract information and note it accurately yet briefly. Encourage the children to search the website more than once.

Assessment evidence
At level 1, the children may need additional reading support, but will often cope well with negotiating a website. They should be able to identify some answers and will have started to understand the concept of notes. At levels 2-3, the children should enjoy using the website with little adult support, and will discover most answers. They will make good use of hot spots and other features. Their note-making should be showing more confidence and skill. This activity will provide evidence towards Reading AF2.

Next steps
Support: If the children struggle to use the website, let them watch you demonstrating it first.
Extension: Challenge the children to design an improved page for the website.

Key aspects of learning
Information processing: Children will identify relevant information from a range of sources on paper and on screen and use this to write their own information texts.

Phase ③ Evaluating resources

Learning outcome
Children can compare and evaluate research material from books and ICT texts.

Success criteria
● I can find information in a non-fiction text.
● I can compare ICT texts and books and evaluate how useful they are.

Setting the context
Ensure the children have already completed the Phase 2 activities – using an information text and a website to find out information about Samuel Pepys. Put the children into pairs and provide them with a copy of the photocopiable page 'The Story of Samuel Pepys' (version 1 or 2) and the previous notes that they wrote on the photocopiable 'Questions about Samuel Pepys'.

Assessment opportunity
Ask partners to tell each other what they thought about the book text. Was it easy to use? Could they find the answers to their questions? What didn't they like about it? Repeat this discussion for the ICT text, providing the access to the website and their notes from the previous activity. Afterwards, give out the photocopiable page 'Comparing sources of information' for the children to write their evaluation and comparison of the two types of research material.

Assessment evidence
At level 1, the children may need to have the printed text re-read to them and the website demonstrated. They should also be able to express simple opinions. At levels 2-3, the children will quickly recall previous work, have interesting discussions and make some perceptive comments on the photocopiable page. This activity will provide evidence towards Reading AF2.

Next steps
Support: If the children struggle with the photocopiable page, provide adult support so that answers can be expressed orally as the adult scribes.
Extension: Challenge the children to design and create a simple website about Samuel Pepys.

Key aspects of learning

Enquiry: Children will ask questions arising from work in another area of the curriculum, research and then plan how to present the information effectively.

Information processing: Children will identify relevant information from a range of sources on paper and on screen and use this to write their own information texts.

Communication: Children will develop their ability to discuss as they work collaboratively in paired, group and whole-class contexts. They will develop their ability to listen critically to broadcast information and to make an oral presentation. They will also communicate outcomes in writing.

Phase ③ Planning research

Learning outcome
Children can pose and record questions for investigation.

Success criteria
● I can ask questions.
● I can write questions.
● I can compare ICT texts and books and evaluate how useful they are.

Setting the context
Ensure the children have seen and used a wide range of information texts, and have already completed the Phase 1 activity 'Asking questions' and both Phase 2 activities. Begin by explaining to the children that they are starting a new history topic – about a man called Edward Jenner. Ask them for suggestions of ways in which they could find out more about him.

Assessment opportunity
Invite the children to write on their individual whiteboards a question word beginning with *Wh-* that they think would be useful. Ask them to share their word with their partner and to think of another *Wh-* word that they could use. Encourage partner discussion, prompting the children to consider the importance of these words when finding out about someone, and the places they might go to find the information they need. Provide the children with a sheet of paper and ask them to list at least six questions that they would like the answers to. Let those working at level 1 complete this with a partner.

Assessment evidence
At level 1, discussion contributions will be brief, but the children should be aware of books and ICT texts as sources of information. With support, they will write questions using some of the starting words they have listed. At levels 2–3, the children will conduct interesting, informed discussions, make suggestions and should cope independently with the task. This activity will provide evidence towards Writing AF1.

Next steps
Support: If the children struggle with the task, guide them towards useful questioning using role play.
Extension: Let the children compare questions with a partner. Ask them to evaluate them, deciding which set of questions is likely to provide answers that give the widest range of information.

Key aspects of learning
Enquiry: Children will ask questions arising from work in another area of the curriculum, research and then plan how to present the information effectively.

NON-FICTION

Periodic assessment

Reading

Learning outcomes
● Children can do research and make notes from books and ICT texts.
● Children can compare and evaluate research material.

Success criteria
● I can find information by using books and ICT texts.
● I can make notes from different non-fiction texts.
● I can compare ICT texts and books and evaluate how useful they are.

Setting the context
Ensure the children have experience of investigating research material in the form of books and ICT texts, and making notes in preparation for writing their own texts. They should also have completed the Phase 3 activity 'Planning research'. Remind the children of the work they did in this activity and revisit the lists of questions that they compiled about Edward Jenner.

Assessment opportunity
Display and give out copies of the photocopiable page 'Non-fiction 3 Reading assessment'. Explain to the children that they are going to be writing their own book about Edward Jenner with specific chapter headings. Give children the photocopiable page 'Non-fiction 3 Reading assessment text' to read and make notes from. Encourage partner reading for help with awkward words, but offer support with unfamiliar vocabulary, particularly at level 1. Progress the children onto the website, www.bbc.co.uk/schools/famouspeople standard/jenner/learn to continue their research.

Assessment evidence
At level 1, the children will need guidance about keeping notes brief and relevant. They will need support with reading text and should be prompted to identify relevant information. They may need an adult to help investigate the website with them, pausing and prompting when they should make notes. At levels 2–3, the children should work with greater independence, but may prefer to discuss information with a partner as they decide whether it is relevant to their chapters. They will often need reminding to keep notes brief and simple, and may need help with the website. This activity will help you judge the children's overall understanding of work in this unit and provide evidence against Reading AF1 and AF2.

Periodic assessment

Writing

Learning outcomes
- Children can use their notes to write a simple information text.
- Children can complete and evaluate a simple information text.

Success criteria
- I can make notes from different non-fiction texts.
- I can use notes to write a simple information text.
- I can create and evaluate an information text.

Setting the context
Children should have completed the Periodic Reading activity prior to this assessment. Return the children's completed 'Non-fiction 3 Reading assessment' from the previous activity and revise their knowledge of Edward Jenner.

Assessment opportunity
Put the children into pairs of comparable ability to talk through their notes. Then, invite them to make a simple, folding (concertina) book. Suggest leaving the cover until after completion, but instruct them to use their chapter headings from the completed photocopiable page for their contents page. As the children start writing their book, remind them of a helpful sequence to follow when writing a chapter:
- Check notes.
- Rehearse wording of sentences (in their heads or with a partner).
- Write the chapter heading and text.
- Consider if a picture and caption may be useful.

If time is available, do this assessment in extended writing sessions during the course of a week. If time is limited to one session, reduce the writing task to one, selected chapter. Afterwards, let partners read each other's texts. Listen as they provide their partner with an oral evaluation. Finish by giving the children the photocopiable page 'Non-fiction 3 Writing assessment' to complete.

Assessment evidence
At level 1, the children will probably need some individual prompting as they revise their notes orally. Their text writing will be brief but should be mainly relevant. At levels 2–3, the children will remember and understand their notes fairly readily. Their writing will be longer, more skilful and include some appropriate layout features. This activity will help you judge the children's overall understanding of work in this unit and provide evidence against Writing AF1 and AF2.

The Story of Samuel Pepys (1)

The boy

Samuel Pepys was born in 1633. He went to a school in London. He did very well at school.

The adult

When he was grown up, he had an important job.
He worked for the Government. He also married a young lady called Elizabeth.

Interests and hobbies

Pepys liked wearing smart clothes. He enjoyed music.
He also enjoyed writing a diary.

What he wrote

In his diary, Pepys wrote about the Great Plague and the Great Fire of London. These were very important events.

Final years

Samuel Pepys died in 1703.

Name	Date

Comparing sources of information

I looked for information about:

_____

The most useful place for information was:

_____

_____

It was the most useful because:

_____

_____

The most interesting information I found was:

_____

_____

I would improve the paper text by:

_____

_____

I would improve the screen text by:

_____

_____

Unit 3 📖 **Information texts**

Red ⬤
Amber ⬤
Green ⬤

I can find information in a non-fiction text. ☐

I can compare ICT texts and books and evaluate how useful they are. ☐

NON-FICTION

NON-FICTION
UNIT 4 Non-chronological reports

Literacy objectives

Speak and listen for a wide range of purposes in different contexts
Strand 1 Speaking
● Explain ideas and processes using imaginative and adventurous vocabulary and non-verbal gestures to support communication.

Read and write for a range of purposes on paper and on screen
Strand 5 Word recognition: decoding (reading) and encoding (spelling)
● Read independently and with increasing fluency longer and less familiar texts.
● Spell with increasing accuracy and confidence, drawing on word recognition and knowledge of word structure, and spelling patterns.
● Know how to tackle unfamiliar words that are not completely decodable.
● Read and spell less common alternative graphemes including trigraphs.
● Read high and medium frequency words independently and automatically.
Strand 6 Word structure and spelling
● Spell with increasing accuracy and confidence, drawing on word recognition and knowledge of word structure, and spelling patterns including common inflections and use of double letters.
● Read and spell less common alternative graphemes including trigraphs.
Strand 7 Understanding and interpreting texts
● Draw together ideas and information from across a whole text, using simple signposts in the text.
● Explain organisational features of texts, including alphabetical order, layout, diagrams, captions, hyperlinks and bullet points.
Strand 8 Engaging with and responding to texts
● Explain their reactions to texts, commenting on important aspects.
Strand 9 Creating and shaping texts
● Select from different presentational features to suit particular writing purposes on paper and on screen.
Strand 10 Text structure and organisation
● Use planning to establish clear sections for writing.
● Use appropriate language to make sections hang together.
Strand 12 Presentation
● Word-process short narrative and non-narrative texts.

Key aspects of learning

Enquiry
● Children will ask questions arising from work in another area of the curriculum, research and then plan how to present the information effectively.
Information processing
● Children will identify relevant information from a range of sources on paper and on screen and use this to write their own non-chronological reports.

Key aspects of learning (continued)

Evaluation
● Children will present information orally and in writing. They will discuss success criteria, give feedback to others and judge the effectiveness of their own work.

Communication
● Children will develop their ability to discuss as they work collaboratively in paired, group and whole-class contexts. They will develop their ability to listen critically to broadcast information and to make an oral presentation. They will also communicate outcomes in writing.

Assessment focuses

Reading
AF2 *(understand, describe, select or retrieve information, events or ideas from texts and use quotation and reference to text).*
AF4 *(identify and comment on the structure and organisation of texts, including grammatical and presentational features at text level).*

Writing
AF4 *(construct paragraphs and use cohesion within and between paragraphs).*

Speaking and listening
Speaking (speak in an organised manner; use detail).

Resources

Phase 1 activities
Photocopiable page, 'Nocturnal animals'
Photocopiable page, 'Reading pathways'
Interactive activity, 'Special features'
Phase 2 activities
Photocopiable page, 'Writing skeleton (a)'
Photocopiable page, 'Nocturnal animals'
Photocopiable page, 'Writing skeleton (b)'
Interactive activity, 'Writing skeleton'
Phase 3 activities
Photocopiable page, 'Feedback comments'
Photocopiable page, 'Writing skeleton (a)'
Periodic assessment
Photocopiable page, 'Non-fiction 4 Reading assessment text (a)'
Photocopiable page, 'Non-fiction 4 Reading assessment'
Interactive activity, 'Non-fiction 4 Reading assessment text (b)'
Photocopiable page, 'Non-fiction 4 Writing assessment'

Unit 4 ⬛ Non-chronological reports

Learning outcomes	Assessment opportunity and evidence	Assessment focuses (AFs)	Success criteria
		Level 1	
Phase ① activities pages 117–118			
Finding pathways • Children can identify the main features of a non-chronological report, including grammatical features and key vocabulary. • Children can read and retrieve information from a non-chronological report.	• Paired activity where children use a non-chronological text to find answers to a series of questions, identify the pathways that helped them and complete an evaluation of the text. • Partner discussion and response to oral questioning. • Children's written answers and evaluation on the photocopiable.	**Reading AF2** • Some simple points from familiar texts recalled. • Some pages/sections of interest located. **Reading AF4** Some awareness of meaning of simple text features.	• I can recognise a non-chronological report. • I can use a non-chronological report to find information.
Retrieving information • Children can identify the main features of a non-chronological report, including grammatical features and key vocabulary. • Children can read and retrieve information from a non-chronological report.	• Paired activity where children complete an interactive, identifying the special features of a non-chronological text, and use an ICT text to answer questions and evaluate it alongside a paper version. • Partner discussion and completion of the interactive activity, and use of the ICT text. • Children's completed evaluation of the paper and ICT text.	**Reading AF2** • Some simple points from familiar texts recalled. • Some pages/sections of interest located.	• I can recognise a non-chronological report. • I can use a non-chronological report to find information.
Phase ② activities pages 119–120			
Reading a writing skeleton • Children can read and understand a writing skeleton. • Children can organise their ideas into general themes, subheadings, key details and information.	• Paired activity where children examine an incomplete writing skeleton, answer questions about how the writer has chosen to organise their plan and complete a writing skeleton. • Group and paired discussion of the writing skeleton, and responses to oral questioning. • Children's completed writing skeletons.	**Reading AF4** Some awareness of meaning of simple text features.	• I can understand a writing skeleton. • I can plan and create a writing skeleton.
Creating a writing skeleton Children can organise their ideas into general themes, subheadings, key details and information.	• Supported paired and group activity where children are given a non-chronological report with a curriculum-linked theme and asked to plan and complete a writing skeleton. • Paired discussion and planning of the writing skeleton. • Children's completed writing skeletons.	**Writing AF4** Simple connections between ideas, events.	• I can understand a writing skeleton. • I can plan and create a writing skeleton.

Unit 4 ☐ Non-chronological reports

Learning outcomes	Assessment opportunity and evidence	Assessment focuses (AFs)	Success criteria
		Level 1	
Phase ③ activities pages 121–122			
Giving feedback Children can evaluate other writing skeletons and use feedback to edit their own skeleton.	• Paired activity where children exchange writing skeletons, evaluate each other's plans and provide feedback comments. • Partner discussion of writing skeletons. • Children's written feedback comments on the photocopiable.	**Reading AF4** Some awareness of meaning of simple text features.	• I can evaluate other skeletons. • I can use feedback to edit my own skeleton.
Using feedback • Children can review, evaluate and give feedback on a draft plan. • Children can listen to and read feedback comments and edit a plan appropriately.	• Group activity where children give oral feedback on each other's draft plan, which is then used to edit and improve the writing skeletons. • Oral feedback and presentation of evaluation notes. • Children's edited writing skeletons.	**Reading AF4** Some awareness of meaning of simple text features.	• I can evaluate other skeletons. • I can give and receive feedback • I can use feedback to edit my own skeleton.

Learning outcomes	Assessment opportunity and evidence	Assessment focuses (AFs)		Success criteria
		Level 2	Level 3	
Phase ① activities pages 117–118				
Finding pathways • Children can identify the main features of a non-chronological report, including grammatical features and key vocabulary. • Children can read and retrieve information from a non-chronological report.	• Independent or paired activity where children use a non-chronological text to find answers to a series of questions, identify the pathways that helped them and complete an evaluation of the text. • Partner discussion and response to oral questioning. • Children's written answers and evaluation on the photocopiable.	**Reading AF4** Some awareness of use of features of organisation.	**Reading AF4** A few basic features of organisation at text level identified, with little or no linked comment.	• I can recognise a non-chronological report. • I can use a non-chronological report to find information.
Retrieving information • Children can identify the main features of a non-chronological report, including grammatical features and key vocabulary. • Children can read and retrieve information from a non-chronological report.	• Paired activity where children complete an interactive, identifying the special features of a non-chronological text, and use an ICT text to answer questions and evaluate it alongside a paper version. • Partner discussion and completion of the interactive activity, and use of the ICT text. • Children's completed evaluation of the paper and ICT text.	**Reading AF2** • Some specific, straightforward information recalled. • Generally clear idea of where to look for information.	**Reading AF2** • Simple, most obvious points identified though there may also be some misunderstanding. • Some comments include quotations from or references to text, but not always relevant.	• I can recognise a non-chronological report. • I can use a non-chronological report to find information. • I can use success criteria to evaluate different texts.

Unit 4 ▣ Non-chronological reports

Learning outcomes	Assessment opportunity and evidence	Assessment focuses (AFs)		Success criteria
		Level 2	Level 3	
Phase ② activities pages 119–120				
Reading a writing skeleton ● Children can read and understand a writing skeleton. ● Children can organise their ideas into general themes, subheadings, key details and information.	● Independent or paired activity where children examine an incomplete writing skeleton, answer questions about how the writer has chosen to organise their plan and complete a writing skeleton. ● Group and paired discussion of the writing skeleton, and responses to oral questioning. ● Children's completed writing skeletons.	**Reading AF4** Some awareness of use of features of organisation.	**Reading AF4** A few basic features of organisation at text level identified, with little or no linked comment.	● I can understand a writing skeleton. ● I can plan and create a writing skeleton.
Creating a writing skeleton Children can organise their ideas into general themes, subheadings, key details and information.	● Paired activity where children are given a non-chronological report with a curriculum-linked theme and asked to plan and complete a writing skeleton. ● Paired discussion and planning of the writing skeleton. ● Children's completed writing skeletons.	**Writing AF4** Ideas in sections grouped by content, some linking by simple pronouns.	**Writing AF4** ● Some internal structure within sections of text. ● Within paragraphs/ sections, some links between sentences. ● Movement between paragraphs/sections sometimes abrupt or disjointed.	● I can understand a writing skeleton. ● I can plan and create a writing skeleton.
Phase ③ activities pages 121–122				
Giving feedback Children can evaluate other writing skeletons and use feedback to edit their own skeleton.	● Paired activity where children exchange writing skeletons, evaluate each other's plans and provide feedback comments. ● Partner discussion of writing skeletons. ● Children's written feedback comments on the photocopiable.	**Reading AF4** Some awareness of use of features of organisation.	**Reading AF4** A few basic features of organisation at text level identified, with little or no linked comment.	● I can evaluate other skeletons. ● I can use feedback to edit my own skeleton
Using feedback ● Children can review, evaluate and give feedback on a draft plan. ● Children can listen to and read feedback comments and edit a plan appropriately.	● Group activity where children give oral feedback on each other's draft plan, which is then used to edit and improve the writing skeletons. ● Independent oral feedback and presentation of evaluation notes. ● Children's edited writing skeletons.	**Reading AF4** Some awareness of use of features of organisation.	**Reading AF4** A few basic features of organisation at text level identified, with little or no linked comment.	● I can evaluate other skeletons. ● I can give and receive feedback. ● I can use feedback to edit my own skeleton.

NON-FICTION

Phase ① Finding pathways

Learning outcomes
● Children can identify the main features of a non-chronological report, including grammatical features and key vocabulary.
● Children can read and retrieve information from a non-chronological report.

Success criteria
● I can recognise a non-chronological report.
● I can use a non-chronological report to find information.

Setting the context
The children should have already had experience of scanning texts for information and offering opinions about the suitability of a text for research. Ensure everyone knows what a non-chronological report is, and is familiar with its main features. Give each child a copy of the photocopiable page 'Nocturnal animals'. Read it together as a class.

Assessment opportunity
Put the children into pairs of comparable ability to re-read the text with a partner. Give everyone four sticky notes to number one to four. Ask four simple, factual questions about the information in the text. For example, *What do owls eat? Where does a badger live?* Number and write the questions on the whiteboard. Invite the children to find the answers to the questions by placing a sticky note on the heading or key word (reading pathway) that helped them. Once all the questions have been asked, give the children the photocopiable page 'Reading pathways' to complete. Repeat the oral and practical activity with those working at level 1, while those working at levels 2–3 pose two new questions for a partner.

Assessment evidence
At level 1, the children should be able to locate some answers from the text, but may need a second try and will rely on partner support. Completion of the photocopiable 'Reading pathways' may prove too difficult, so base assessment on their spoken answers and placing of the sticky notes. At levels 2–3, the children should do most of the task independently and understand the benefit of the reading pathways. They may prefer to work with a partner, but will record in writing on their own photocopiable 'Reading pathways'. This activity will provide evidence towards Reading AF2 and AF4.

Next steps
Support: If the children struggle with the task, provide adult support, pointing to the feature or key word leading to the information.
Extension: Suggest the children compare their answer sheets and the location of their sticky notes with a partner's results, looking to see if their reading pathways differ.

Key aspects of learning
Information processing: Children will identify relevant information from a range of sources on paper and on screen and use this to write their own non-chronological reports.
Evaluation: Children will present information orally and in writing. They will discuss success criteria, give feedback to others and judge the effectiveness of their own work.

NON-FICTION

Phase ① Retrieving information

Learning outcomes
● Children can identify the main features of a non-chronological report, including grammatical features and key vocabulary.
● Children can read and retrieve information from a non-chronological report.

Success criteria
● I can recognise a non-chronological report.
● I can use a non-chronological report to find information.

Setting the context
Prior to this assessment, the children should already be familiar with different types of non-fiction texts and their main features, and have experience of reading paper and ICT non-chronological reports. Ensure everybody has completed the previous activity.

Assessment opportunity
Put the children into pairs and give them the interactive activity 'Special features'. Next, give the children the photocopiable page 'Nocturnal animals' and ask them to read the text in order to answer the questions on the interactive activity. Encourage partners to discuss each set of possible answers before they make a selection. Once the screens have been completed, ask children to print off their results.

Assessment evidence
At level 1, the children will often guess answers to the questions and will need to repeat the interactive activity several times. At levels 2–3, the children should engage in more thoughtful discussions and select answers carefully, but they will not always be correct. This activity will provide evidence towards Reading AF2.

Next steps
Support: If the children struggle to use the online text, limit their investigation to two or three animals. If necessary, accept an oral evaluation.
Extension: Put the children into small groups to make an oral presentation of their evaluation to one another.

Key aspects of learning
Information processing: Children will identify relevant information from a range of sources on paper and on screen and use this to write their own non-chronological reports.
Evaluation: Children will present information orally and in writing. They will discuss success criteria, give feedback to others and judge the effectiveness of their own work.
Communication: Children will develop their ability to discuss as they work collaboratively in paired, group and whole-class contexts. They will develop their ability to listen critically to broadcast information and to make an oral presentation. They will also communicate outcomes in writing.

Phase ② Reading a writing skeleton

Learning outcomes
● Children can read and understand a writing skeleton.
● Children can organise their ideas into general themes, subheadings, key details and information.

Success criteria
● I can understand a writing skeleton.
● I can plan and create a writing skeleton.

Setting the context
Ensure the children have seen and used writing plans, in particular writing skeletons. Familiarise them with the term 'key interests' to refer to the main areas of writing in a non-chronological report. Display the photocopiable page 'Writing skeleton (a)' and explain that it shows an incomplete writing plan for a non-chronological report about nocturnal animals.

Assessment opportunity
Give the children individual copies of the plan and put them into pairs to discuss it. Use oral questioning to assess their understanding, getting them to respond by pointing to sections of the plan or writing answers on their whiteboard. For example, *Point to a key interest. Point to the subject of the report. How many sections will there be when all the planning is done? How many sections are planned at the moment? Write one of the subheadings for the report. Show me a reading pathway.* Afterwards, explain that the writer has left this skeleton unfinished. Ask the children to finish the skeleton, filling in the blank spaces for the writer. Suggest that they write in rough first, using copies of the photocopiable page 'Nocturnal animals' (from the previous activity) to help with ideas.

Assessment evidence
At level 1, the children may need support, working as a group with you to discuss the skeleton and watching as you first demonstrate answers to your questions. With support, they should be able to complete a new section of the skeleton. At levels 2–3, the children should understand the structure and logic of the skeleton. They may discuss new sections for the skeleton with a partner, but should be able to complete most of the skeleton independently. This activity will provide evidence towards Reading AF4.

Next steps
Support: If the children struggle to complete the photocopiable page, provide adult support, talking through ideas and collaborating on simple writing.
Extension: Suggest the children add further details to each section of the skeleton.

Key aspects of learning
Enquiry: Children will ask questions arising from work in another area of the curriculum, research and then plan how to present the information effectively.
Communication: Children will develop their ability to discuss as they work collaboratively in paired, group and whole-class contexts. They will develop their ability to listen critically to broadcast information and to make an oral presentation. They will also communicate outcomes in writing.

NON-FICTION

Phase ② Creating a writing skeleton

Learning outcome
Children can organise their ideas into general themes, subheadings, key details and information.

Success criteria
- I can understand a writing skeleton.
- I can plan and create a writing skeleton.

Setting the context
The children should have already completed the previous activity. If necessary, remind them of what they did and look back at their finished writing skeletons. Explain that they are now going to be writing a skeleton for a new non-chronological report.

Assessment opportunity
Put children into pairs. Decide on a curriculum-linked theme for the skeletons, such as plants, animals, the seaside, healthy eating or people who help us. Encourage children to plan their skeleton in rough first before progressing to the photocopiable page 'Writing skeleton (b)'. For those working at level 1, put four or five pairs into a group, with adult support, to discuss the content of a new, complete writing skeleton. The adult can then allocate one or two sections for each pair to work on.

Assessment evidence
At level 1, the children will need reminding about the layout and meaning of a writing skeleton, and will need the support of an adult-led group to think of content ideas. They should be able to complete one or two sections of the collaborative skeleton. At levels 2–3, the children will remember and understand previous work on writing skeletons and should engage in useful discussion with a partner to plan and write a new skeleton. They may sometimes need confirmation that they are allocating information correctly. This activity will provide evidence towards Writing AF4.

Next steps
Support: If the children struggle, limit their contribution to planning a single section.
Extension: Challenge the children to create a writing skeleton for another topic area using the interactive activity 'Writing skeleton'.

Key aspects of learning
Enquiry: Children will ask questions arising from work in another area of the curriculum, research and then plan how to present the information effectively.
Evaluation: Children will present information orally and in writing. They will discuss success criteria, give feedback to others and judge the effectiveness of their own work.
Communication: Children will develop their ability to discuss as they work collaboratively in paired, group and whole-class contexts. They will develop their ability to listen critically to broadcast information and to make an oral presentation. They will also communicate outcomes in writing.

Phase ③ Giving feedback

Success criteria
- I can evaluate other skeletons.
- I can use feedback to edit my own skeleton.

Setting the context
Ensure the children have experience of looking at and providing feedback on a peer's work. They should have already done the previous activity and produced a writing skeleton for a new topic area.

Assessment opportunity
Put the children into the same pairs as before and return their writing skeletons. Suggest everybody checks their writing skeletons first, to make sure that they are happy with their planning. Then, let each pair exchange their skeletons with another pair. Listen to partner discussion as the children orally review and evaluate the other pair's writing skeleton. Listen as they talk about whether the planned pathways and text organisation are effective. Then give each child a copy of the photocopiable page 'Feedback comments' to write an evaluation. Suggest they write notes rather than sentences.

Assessment evidence
At level 1, the children's written comments will be simple. At levels 2–3, the children will show greater understanding of the skeleton, and should notice planned reading pathways. Their written feedback should have some constructive comments about text organisation and suggested improvement. This activity will provide evidence towards Reading AF4.

Next steps
Support: If the children struggle to complete written feedback, provide adult support to act as a scribe.
Extension: Suggest the children evaluate the incomplete 'Writing skeleton (a)' (from Phase 2).

Key aspects of learning
Evaluation: Children will present information orally and in writing. They will discuss success criteria, give feedback to others and judge the effectiveness of their own work.
Communication: Children will develop their ability to discuss as they work collaboratively in paired, group and whole-class contexts. They will develop their ability to listen critically to broadcast information and to make an oral presentation. They will also communicate outcomes in writing.

NON-FICTION

Phase ③ Using feedback

Learning outcomes
● Children can review, evaluate and give feedback on a draft plan.
● Children can listen to and read feedback comments and edit a plan appropriately.

Success criteria
● I can evaluate other skeletons.
● I can give and receive feedback.
● I can use feedback to edit my own skeleton.

Setting the context
Ensure the children have already completed the previous two activities. Return the 'Feedback comments' from the previous activity and provide time for the children to remind themselves of what they wrote.

Assessment opportunity
Put the children back into the same groups as before. Ask each child to give oral feedback to the creators of the skeleton that they evaluated previously. Remind them to use their written notes as a prompt. As the children give feedback, listen to the vocabulary used, assessing their awareness of the need to plan reading pathways and to plan a non-chronological report that is clearly divided into key interests and contains specific details. Afterwards, suggest writing partners discuss the feedback they have received and edit their skeletons where necessary.

Assessment evidence
At level 1, the children will need reminding about the previous task and will need support in discussing and presenting their comments. Writers will make some use of the feedback by simple editing of their skeleton. At levels 2–3, the children will quickly remember the task and understand their notes. They should make some constructive comments to the writers and be able to justify their feedback. Writers will make good use of constructive feedback to edit their skeleton appropriately. (Save these completed skeletons for use in the Periodic Reading activity.) This activity will provide evidence towards Reading AF4.

Next steps
Support: If needed, provide adult support, helping both speakers and listeners in the process. Prompt children with suggested editing.
Extension: Suggest the children consult a reviewer after editing, to find out if improvements are obvious.

Key aspects of learning
Evaluation: Children will present information orally and in writing. They will discuss success criteria, give feedback to others and judge the effectiveness of their own work.

Periodic assessment

Reading

Learning outcome
Children can identify and evaluate non-chronological reports, using the text layout features to find information.

Success criteria
- I can recognise a non-chronological report.
- I can use a non-chronological report to find information.
- I can use success criteria to evaluate different texts.

Setting the context
Ensure the children have read a variety of non-chronological reports and are familiar with different layouts. They should have experience of finding information in the texts, and have realised that the writer has created helpful reading pathways. The class should have worked together to create a list of success criteria for an effective non-chronological report and it should be displayed.

Assessment opportunity
Give everyone a copy of the photocopiable page 'Non-fiction 4 Reading assessment text (a)' to partner-read and discuss, and a copy of 'Non-fiction 4 Reading assessment' to complete. Let those working at level 1 collaborate with a partner and have adult support in reading the questions. Encourage children working at levels 2–3 to work with greater independence, sometimes conferring with a partner to compare ideas as they look for information. Be aware of individual contributions to any discussion. Afterwards, ask the children to complete the interactive activity 'Non-fiction 4 Reading assessment text (b)', working on it in pairs. Watch and listen as partners search the text and discuss whether information is easier or harder to understand.

Assessment evidence
At level 1, the children will need support when reading the text and writing their answers. They may only be able to show you how they found information as opposed to expressing it in words. They will cope with investigating the interactive activity and will be able to write, with support, some simple comments on the evaluation sheet. At levels 2–3, the children should read and respond to the text competently. They will make good use of the interactive text and should make a perceptive evaluation. This activity will help you judge the children's overall understanding of work in this unit and provide evidence against Reading AF2 and AF4.

NON-FICTION

Periodic assessment

Writing

Learning outcomes
- Children can write a non-chronological report on a theme, using subheadings, key details and information to structure the text.
- Children can evaluate non-chronological reports, expressing their views clearly and using evidence from the text.

Success criteria
- I can plan and create a writing skeleton.
- I can write my own non-chronological report.
- I can evaluate my own non-chronological report.

Setting the context
Ensure the children have experience of writing non-chronological reports and evaluating them against established success criteria. Remind the children of the Phase 3 activity 'Using feedback' and the work leading up to it. Pair children with their writing partners from the Phase 3 activity, and return their completed skeletons (see page 119).

Assessment opportunity
Encourage partners to discuss the skeleton, reminding themselves of their plan. Explain that they are now going to use their skeleton to help them write a non-chronological report. If possible, let children use computers so they can type their text and make changes more easily. At level 1, let partners work together on one or two paragraphs allocated to them. With adult support, this text can then be combined with other pairs' work to form one non-chronological report. At levels 2-3, most of the children will assume control of an independent report. If necessary, keep partners together to share the task, each working on some sections on screen and using each other as a response partner. Afterwards, give children the photocopiable page 'Non-fiction 4 Writing assessment' to self-assess their work.

Assessment evidence
At level 1, the children will need help remembering the task and the purpose of the writing skeleton. They will need the support of a writing partner, but should be able to contribute a subheading and a paragraph to the report, and complete a simple self-assessment. At levels 2-3, the children will understand their task and should work without adult support. If working with a partner, they should be able to allocate sections independently, and work on these with a clear understanding of how the finished report will come together. Their self-assessment will provide some thoughtful, perceptive comments. This activity will help you judge the children's overall understanding of work in this unit and provide evidence against Writing AF4 and AF7.

Nocturnal animals

Nocturnal animals are active at night. Many of these nocturnal animals live in the woodlands as it can be a good place to hunt for food at night.

NON-FICTION

Bats

The common British bat often lives in a forest. This nocturnal animal flies around at night, searching for food. It makes a squeaking sound as it flies. The sound and their big ears help the animal work out direction. During the day, the bat hangs upside down to sleep.

Toads

The toad can live in water and on land. This nocturnal animal hunts on land for its food. At night, it catches its food with its long, sticky tongue. The toad likes to eat flies, beetles and spiders.

Badgers

The badger is a large animal that can grow up to one metre long. It lives in an underground home called a sett. This nocturnal animal hunts for insects, and uses its long claws to dig for fruit and roots.

Owls

The owl flies around at night, using its huge eyes to watch for food. This nocturnal animal flies so quietly that its prey does not hear it. The owl eats mice, beetles and small birds.

Foxes

The fox is a nocturnal animal that can be found in many different environments. During the day, it lives in a home called an earth. At night, it comes above ground and often goes in search of small farm animals as food.

Bat © Craig Dingle/www.istockphoto.com; toad © FLPA/Paul Hobson/Holt; badger © 2009, photolibrary.com; owl © www.istockphoto.com; fox © 2009, photolibrary.com; fox © Eric Gevart/www.istockphoto.com.

Name _____   Date _____

Reading pathways

~~~~~~

Question _____

Answer _____

Layout or text feature that helped me _____

How effective was this pathway?   good ◯   fair ◯   poor ◯

~~~~~~

Question _____

Answer _____

Layout or text feature that helped me _____

How effective was this pathway?   good ◯   fair ◯   poor ◯

~~~~~~

Question _____

Answer _____

Layout or text feature that helped me _____

How effective was this pathway?   good ◯   fair ◯   poor ◯

~~~~~~

Question _____

Answer _____

Layout or text feature that helped me _____

How effective was this pathway?   good ◯   fair ◯   poor ◯

Red ◯
Amber ◯   I can use a non-chronological report to find information. ☐
Green ◯

Non-fiction 4 Reading assessment text (a)

Getting to school

How children get to school is important. It affects not only the children themselves, but also other people living in the area. There are many different ways children make this journey.

Bicycle

Some children get to school by riding their bicycle. However, roads are busy and many parents feel this is a dangerous way to travel. Wearing a helmet and passing a special cycling test helps make children safer.

Car

Using a car is a very popular way to get to school. Some parents think it is the safest way for their children to travel. Extra cars make the roads very crowded and journeys can be slow.

School bus

There are school buses in country areas. These buses go to local villages, collecting the children. The children can be certain there will always be a seat on the bus for them. The bus takes them right to the school.

Public bus

Some pupils get to school by using public buses. These buses run more often. However, sometimes a bus may be full of other passengers. Then it will go straight past the bus stop where a child is waiting. The bus only stops where there is a bus stop sign, and there may not be one near the school.

Walking

Walking is free. Many children walk to school if their journey is short. Walking is also good exercise. Crossing busy roads is sometimes a problem, so some adults and children walk in a group called a walking bus.

Photo © Ian Miles / Flashpoint Pictures / Alamy.

POETRY

UNIT 1 Patterns on the page

Literacy objectives

Speak and listen for a wide range of purposes in different contexts
Strand 1 Speaking
● Speak with clarity and use appropriate intonation when reading and reciting texts.
Strand 2 Listening and responding
● Respond to presentations by describing characters, repeating some highlights and commenting constructively.
Strand 3 Group discussion and interaction
● Ensure that everyone contributes, allocate tasks, and consider alternatives and reach agreement.
● Work effectively in groups by ensuring that each group member takes a turn challenging, supporting and moving on.
● Listen to each other's views and preferences, agree the next steps to take and identify contributions by each group member.
Strand 4 Drama
● Consider how mood and atmosphere are created in live or recorded performance.

Read and write for a range of purposes on paper and on screen
Strand 5 Word recognition: decoding (reading) and encoding (spelling)
● Read independently and with increasing fluency longer and less familiar texts.
● Spell with increasing accuracy and confidence, drawing on word recognition and knowledge of word structure, and spelling patterns.
● Know how to tackle unfamiliar words that are not completely decodable.
● Read and spell less common alternative graphemes including trigraphs.
● Read high and medium frequency words independently and automatically.
Strand 6 Word structure and spelling
● Spell with increasing accuracy and confidence, drawing on word recognition and knowledge of word structures and spelling patterns including common inflections and use of double letters.
● Read and spell less common alternative graphemes including trigraphs.
Strand 7 Understanding and interpreting texts
● Explore how particular words are used, including words and expressions with similar meanings.
Strand 8 Engaging with and responding to texts
● Explain their reactions to texts, commenting on important aspects.
Strand 9 Creating and shaping texts
● Draw on knowledge and experience of texts in deciding and planning what and how to write.
● Make adventurous word and language choices appropriate to the style and purpose of the text.
● Select from different presentational features to suit particular writing purposes on paper and on screen.
Strand 12 Presentation
● Write legibly, using upper and lower case letters appropriately within words, and observing correct spacing within and between words.
● Form and use the four basic handwriting joins.
● Word-process short narrative and non-narrative texts.

Key aspects of learning

Reasoning
- Children will explain the ways in which poems are patterned and how those patterns could be continued or varied.

Communication
- Children will begin to develop their ability to discuss patterns in the poetry and to create their own using carefully chosen words and phrases. They will sometimes work collaboratively in pairs and groups. They will communicate outcomes orally and in writing (possibly including ICT).

Assessment focuses

Reading
AF4 (identify and comment on the structure and organisation of texts, including grammatical and presentational features at text level).
AF5 (explain and comment on writers' use of language, including grammatical and literary features at word and sentence level).

Writing
AF2 (produce texts which are appropriate to task, reader and purpose).
AF7 (select appropriate and effective vocabulary).

Speaking and listening
Speaking (speak with clarity, intonation and pace).
Listening and responding (listen to others; ask relevant questions; follow instructions).
Group discussion and interaction (take turns).
Drama (evaluate performances).

Resources

Phase 1 activities
Photocopiable page, 'B, Beautiful B'
Photocopiable page, 'Hearing patterns'
Photocopiable page, 'Seeing patterns'
Phase 2 activities
Interactive activity, 'Playing with patterns'
Photocopiable page, 'Playing with patterns'
Photocopiable page, 'Squeezes'
Photocopiable page, 'Waves'
Phase 3 activities
Photocopiable page, 'The Clown's Last Joke'
Photocopiable page, 'Inside the clown's box
Interactive activity, 'Sound patterns'
Periodic assessment
Photocopiable page, 'Poetry 1 Reading assessment text'
Photocopiable page, 'Poetry 1 Reading assessment (a)'
Interactive activity, 'Poetry1 Reading assessment (b)'

Unit 1 ▢ Patterns on the page

Learning outcomes	Assessment opportunity and evidence	Assessment focuses (AFs)	Success criteria
		Level 1	

Phase ① activities pages 133-134

Learning outcomes	Assessment opportunity and evidence	Assessment focuses (AFs) Level 1	Success criteria
Hearing patterns Children can listen to, read and perform poems, identifying different patterns in their language use and structure.	● Paired and group activity where children listen to a poem, identify the language patterns used and plan and present an oral performance of the poem. ● Partner discussion, role play and presentation of the poem. ● Children's written responses on the photocopiable.	**Reading AF5** Comments on obvious features of language.	● I can find patterns in poetry. ● I can plan and put on a poetry performance.
Seeing patterns Children can listen to, read and perform poems, identifying different patterns in their language use and structure.	● Paired and group activity where children look at a poem, comment on the visual structure of the language and perform the poem to an audience. ● Partner discussion and group performance of the poem. ● Children's written responses on the photocopiable.	**Reading AF4** Some awareness of meaning of simple text features.	● I can find patterns in poetry. ● I can plan and put on a poetry performance.

Phase ② activities pages 135-136

Learning outcomes	Assessment opportunity and evidence	Assessment focuses (AFs) Level 1	Success criteria
Playing with patterns Children understand how to play with interesting and inventive language choices to create or continue particular patterns.	● Paired activity where children identify alliterative patterns in a poem. ● Partner discussion while completing both screens of the interactive activity.	**Reading AF5** Comments on obvious features of language.	I can continue a word pattern.
Making patterns Children know how to go about writing a pattern or shape poem of their own.	● Paired activity where children listen to a shape poem, suggest how it might be presented on the page and adapt an existing poem into a shape poem. ● Partner discussion and oral responses. ● Children's completed shape poems.	**Writing AF7** ● Mostly simple vocabulary. ● Communicates meaning through repetition of key words.	● I can recognise a shape poem. ● I can create a shape poem.

Unit 1 📖 Patterns on the page

Learning outcomes	Assessment opportunity and evidence	Assessment focuses (AFs)	Success criteria
		Level 1	

Phase ③ activities pages 136-137

Learning outcomes	Assessment opportunity and evidence	Assessment focuses (AFs) Level 1	Success criteria
Playing with words Children can write a simple poem of their own, playing with interesting and inventive language choices to create or continue a particular pattern.	• Independent or paired activity where children play a simple listening game in response to a poem, identify patterns and add their own words and lines to the poem. • Individual responses to the oral game and group discussion of the poem's tone. • Children's item lists and added verses.	**Writing AF7** • Mostly simple vocabulary. • Communicates meaning through repetition of key words.	I can play with words to create patterns in poetry.
Planning patterned poetry Children can write a simple poem of their own, playing with interesting and inventive language choices to create or continue a particular pattern.	• Independent activity where children are asked to complete a birthday present list, adding items that are alliterative. • Individual responses to oral questioning. • Children's completed present lists and interactive activity.	**Writing AF2** Some indication of basic purpose, particular form or awareness of reader.	I can play with words to create patterns in poetry.

Learning outcomes	Assessment opportunity and evidence	Assessment focuses (AFs)		Success criteria
		Level 2	Level 3	

Phase ① activities pages 133-134

Learning outcomes	Assessment opportunity and evidence	Level 2	Level 3	Success criteria
Hearing patterns Children can listen to, read and perform poems, identifying different patterns in their language use and structure.	• Paired and group activity where children listen to a poem, identify the language patterns used and plan and present an oral performance of the poem. • Partner discussion, role play and presentation of the poem. • Children's written responses on the photocopiable.	**Reading AF5** • Some effective language choices noted. • Some familiar patterns of language identified.	**Reading AF5** A few basic features of writer's language identified, but with little or no comment.	• I can find patterns in poetry. • I can plan and put on a poetry performance.
Seeing patterns Children can listen to, read and perform poems, identifying different patterns in their language use and structure.	• Paired and group activity where children look at a poem, comment on the visual structure of the language and perform the poem to an audience. • Partner discussion and group performance of the poem. • Children's written responses on the photocopiable.	**Reading AF4** Some awareness of use of features of organisation.	**Reading AF4** A few basic features of organisation at text level identified, with little or no linked comment.	• I can find patterns in poetry. • I can plan and put on a poetry performance.

Unit 1 🔲 Patterns on the page

Learning outcomes	Assessment opportunity and evidence	Assessment focuses (AFs)		Success criteria
		Level 2	Level 3	
Phase ② activities pages 135-136				
Playing with patterns Children understand how to play with interesting and inventive language choices to create or continue particular patterns.	• Paired activity where children identify alliterative patterns in a poem. • Partner discussion while completing the interactive activity and the photocopiable.	**Reading AF5** • Some effective language choices noted. • Some familiar patterns of language identified.	**Reading AF5** A few basic features of writer's language identified, but with little or no comment.	I can continue a word pattern.
Making patterns Children know how to go about writing a pattern or shape poem of their own.	• Paired and independent activity where children listen to a shape poem, suggest how it might be presented on the page and adapt an existing poem into a shape poem. • Partner discussion and oral responses. • Children's completed shape poems	**Writing AF7** • Simple, often speech-like vocabulary conveys relevant meanings. • Some adventurous word choices.	**Writing AF7** • Simple, generally appropriate vocabulary used, limited in range. • Some words selected for effect or occasion.	• I can recognise a shape poem. • I can create a shape poem.
Phase ③ activities pages 136-137				
Playing with words Children can write a simple poem of their own, playing with interesting and inventive language choices to create or continue a particular pattern.	• Independent or paired activity where children play a simple listening game in response to a poem, identify patterns and add their own words and lines to the poem. • Individual responses to the oral game and group discussion of the poem's tone. • Children's item lists and added verses.	**Writing AF7** • Simple, often speech-like vocabulary conveys relevant meanings. • Some adventurous word choices.	**Writing AF7** • Simple, generally appropriate vocabulary used, limited in range. • Some words selected for effect or occasion.	I can play with words to create patterns in poetry.
Planning patterned poetry Children can write a simple poem of their own, playing with interesting and inventive language choices to create or continue a particular pattern.	• Independent activity where children are asked to complete a birthday present list, adding items that are alliterative. • Individual responses to oral questioning. • Children's completed present lists and interactive activity.	**Writing AF2** • Some basic purpose established. • Some appropriate features of the given form used. • Some attempts to adopt appropriate style.	**Writing AF2** • Purpose established at a general level. • Main features of selected form sometimes signalled to the reader. • Some attempts at appropriate style, with attention to reader.	I can play with words to create patterns in poetry.

Phase ① Hearing patterns

Learning outcome
Children can listen to, read and perform poems, identifying different patterns in their language use and structure.

Success criteria
- I can find patterns in poetry.
- I can plan and put on a poetry performance.

Setting the context
Prior to this assessment, the children should have had the opportunity to hear and read aloud poems with sound patterns. Perform this activity in small groups so that you can overhear partner discussion and assess the children's speaking, listening and interaction skills. Tell the group that you are going to read them a poem with patterns. Invite them to tell a partner what a pattern is.

Assessment opportunity
Divide the group into pairs of comparable ability. Read aloud the unseen poem 'B, Beautiful B!' from the photocopiable page. Invite partners to describe to each other the patterns that they heard. Read it again so partners can share further observations. Then, provide everyone with the photocopiable page 'Hearing patterns' to complete. Afterwards, use the poem for partner role play. One child is the 'radio poetry reader' who reads aloud the poem to their partner, who is the 'audience'. The audience should close their eyes and listen as the poem is read to them. Then let the children swap roles. Progress to partners planning and performing the poem together, with other children of similar ability playing the part of the audience.

Assessment evidence
At level 1, the children will identify simple features such as the repeated sound and focus on animals. They may need the photocopiable page read to them, responding with oral answers. At levels 2–3, the children will use their experience of poetry patterns to comment on repeated words, sounds and alliterative animal names. They will interact with their partner and complete the photocopiable page independently. They will read the poem with expression and listen attentively. This activity will provide evidence towards Reading AF5.

Next steps
Support: If the children struggle with the photocopiable page, present it orally, scribing their answers. Suggest partners perform only one verse, read with support.
Extension: Let partners make an audio recording of their performance for later self-evaluation.

Key aspects of learning
Reasoning: Children will explain the ways in which poems are patterned and how those patterns could be continued or varied.

POETRY

Phase ① Seeing patterns

Learning outcome
Children can listen to, read and perform poems, identifying different patterns in their language use and structure.

Success criteria
● I can find patterns in poetry.
● I can plan and put on a poetry performance.

Setting the context
The children will need to have examined poems with visual patterns and to have completed the previous activity. Perform this assessment with the same groups as before. Explain to the children that they are now going to look at a poem with patterns that they can see.

Assessment opportunity
In pairs, ask the children to remind each other of what a pattern is and how poets can use patterns to present a poem on the page. Prompt them with questions to consider: *How are poems divided? When do poets start new lines? Can punctuation be special? Does every poem have a pattern?* Provide children with the poem 'B, Beautiful B!' (from the previous activity) and the photocopiable page 'Seeing patterns', encouraging further partner discussion as they respond to the questions. Afterwards, put children into larger groups of four or six, to plan and perform the poem to yourself or other groups.

Assessment evidence
At level 1, the children will recognise a poem's division into lines and verses of the same length. They may need the photocopiable page read to them, responding with oral answers. At levels 2–3, the children will comment on lines, regular verses and the repeated pattern of *I'm a...*. Many will spot punctuation patterns and a verse's pattern of lengthening lines. They will interact with others to perform the poem with expression, fluency and understanding and use appropriate actions and body language. This activity will provide evidence towards Reading AF4.

Next steps
Support: If the children struggle with the photocopiable, present it orally, scribing their answers. Prompt ideas with oral questions. For example: *How many lines in the first part? What is the first word in the poem? What is the first word in the second verse? Can you guess how the third verse begins?* Support partner rather than group performance, and model actions.
Extension: Suggest the children add another verse to the poem, following the established patterns.

Key aspects of learning
Reasoning: Children will explain the ways in which poems are patterned and how those patterns could be continued or varied.
Communication: Children will begin to develop their ability to discuss patterns in the poetry and to create their own using carefully chosen words and phrases. They will sometimes work collaboratively in pairs and groups. They will communicate outcomes orally and in writing (possibly including ICT).

Phase ② Playing with patterns

Learning outcome
Children understand how to play with interesting and inventive language choices to create or continue particular patterns.

Success criteria
I can identify a word pattern.

Setting the context
The children should have experience of identifying alliterative patterns. They should have played with continuing patterns, recognising the need to sometimes be inventive in word selection.

Assessment opportunity
Give the children the first screen of the interactive activity 'Playing with patterns'. Ask them to work in pairs on one line of the poem at a time, identifying and highlighting the two words that make a pattern. Afterwards, listen to their explanation of the pattern.

Assessment evidence
At level 1, the children will recognise the use of a repeated first letter and should be able to explain the pattern. At levels 2–3, the children will be able to complete the photocopiable page using a wide range of imaginative and alliterative words. Use the activity to provide evidence towards Reading AF5.

Next steps
Support: For the children who struggle with reading the poem, support them by reading lines aloud with them. Give later prompts, for example: *Look at first letters.*
Extension: Give the children copies of the photocopiable page 'Playing with patterns' to think of their own words to complete each line. Emphasise adventurous or invented language, encouraging preliminary drafts. Invite them to tell you about any other patterns that they can find in the poem. (Repetition of the word *waves*.)

Key aspects of learning
Reasoning: Children will explain the ways in which poems are patterned and how those patterns could be continued or varied.
Communication: Children will begin to develop their ability to discuss patterns in the poetry and to create their own using carefully chosen words and phrases. They will sometimes work collaboratively in pairs and groups. They will communicate outcomes orally and in writing (possibly including ICT).

Phase ② Making patterns

Learning outcome
Children know how to go about writing a pattern or shape poem of their own.

Success criteria
● I can recognise a shape poem.
● I can create a shape poem.

Setting the context
Ensure the children have seen and read shape poems and seen the connections between shape, subject matter and word meaning. The children should have worked with you to create their own shape poems, based on a model provided.

Assessment opportunity
Put the children into pairs of comparable ability. Read aloud the unseen poem 'Squeezes' from the photocopiable page. Ask the children to discuss the poem's pattern with their partner. Prompt with questioning: *How many lines do you think there are? Where do they begin and end? Do you think the poem has a pattern?* Re-read the poem if necessary. Then ask the children if they can visualise what the

POETRY

poem might look like on the page. After partners have compared mental pictures, display the poem on the whiteboard. Ask: *What is the first pattern you notice?* Let children answer your question with a word or drawing held up on their individual whiteboards. (Its shape). Next, give the children a copy of the poem 'Waves', either in its original form on the photocopiable page or their personalised version from the previous activity. Challenge them to create an effective shape poem from it. Suggest making a rough draft first.

Assessment evidence
At level 1, the children will identify that the poem's layout is unusual and they will understand the relevance of the shape to the poem's subject matter. At levels 2-3, the children's oral answers will be more assured. They will work on the poem 'Waves' independently, and their chosen shape is likely to show more detailed connections with the poem's meaning. For example, the first line may have larger letters than the second line. Use this activity to provide evidence towards Writing AF7.

Next steps
Support: For the children who fail to understand the relevance of the poem's shape to its title and words, prompt them to use their hands to mime the movement of a wave before they can go on to create their shape poems.
Extension: Suggest the children use the 'three stars and a wish' technique in their evaluation of a partner's shape poem, identifying three reasons why the shape poem is effective and suggesting one way to improve their next shape poem.

Key aspects of learning
Communication: Children will begin to develop their ability to discuss patterns in the poetry and to create their own using carefully chosen words and phrases. They will sometimes work collaboratively in pairs and groups. They will communicate outcomes orally and in writing (possibly including ICT).

Phase ③ Playing with words

Learning outcome
Children can write a simple poem of their own, playing with interesting and inventive language choices to create or continue a particular pattern.

Success criteria
I can play with words to create patterns in poetry.

Setting the context
Prior to this assessment, the children will need to have seen and heard poems that follow a pattern or structure, and have had the opportunity to use language playfully when responding to a poem.

Assessment opportunity
Assess the children's understanding by doing the first part of this activity in small groups. Give everyone two signs to hold up: 'serious' and 'playful'. Discuss what the words mean. Read aloud the poem 'The Clown's Last Joke' from the photocopiable page. After reading the poem, ask the children to react using the appropriate sign and facial language. Ask them to justify their choices. Now display the poem on the whiteboard. Ask: *Can you point out words or phrases that seem funny?* (*Grinning shoe.*) *Can you find patterns?* (*They found* at the beginning of many lines.) Ask them to think of another four possessions for the clown and list them on the photocopiable page 'Inside the clown's box'. Have them put the items into four new lines for the poem, and decide where in the poem they would place the lines.

Assessment evidence
At level 1, the children will recognise that a clown's possessions are funny and that the poem has a pattern. They will think of and record, through writing or drawing, four more possible possessions for the clown. They may do this individually or working with a partner. At levels 2-3, the children may identify additional patterns. For example, couplets, occasional single lines and repetition of the word *But*. They

will be able to work on four new lines, individually or with a partner, and will have reasoned ideas about their position in the poem. The completed activity will provide evidence towards Writing AF7.

Next steps
Support: For children who struggle for ideas, prompt them with questions. For example, *Did the clown wear a jacket? Could he have a strange tie?*
Extension: Set the task of giving the items an unlikely or interesting characteristic, so readers will not take them too seriously.

Key aspects of learning
Reasoning: Children will explain the ways in which poems are patterned and how those patterns could be continued or varied.
Communication: Children will begin to develop their ability to discuss patterns in the poetry and to create their own using carefully chosen words and phrases. They will sometimes work collaboratively in pairs and groups. They will communicate outcomes orally and in writing (possibly including ICT).

Phase ③ Planning patterned poetry

Learning outcome
Children can write a simple poem of their own, playing with interesting and inventive language choices to create or continue a particular pattern.

Success criteria
I can play with words to create patterns in poetry.

Setting the context
Ensure the children have read many light-hearted poems in which the poet plays with language, in particular to create alliterative patterns. Begin the assessment by telling the children that you are making a birthday list. Write on the whiteboard two unusual presents that you would like for your birthday. Ensure that each item contains an example of alliteration. For example, *a rushing robot, a talking teddy* and so on.

Assessment opportunity
Use oral questioning to assess the children's perception of language patterns. Ask: *Do both presents have a pattern? What is the pattern? Which sounds make the pattern?* Invite the children to create their own present lists, choosing ten interesting and wacky items. Remind them to follow the alliterative pattern that you started on the whiteboard. As they perform the task, encourage re-reading, editing and amending of their notes, before they write their final decisions in list form.

Assessment evidence
At level 1, the children will hear and see the alliteration shown, think of presents and will manage many examples of alliteration. At levels 2–3, the children will spot alliteration more quickly and identify the inventive, interesting vocabulary. They will be more inventive in their list of unusual, alliterative presents. This activity will provide evidence towards Writing AF2.

Next steps
Support: For the children who do not identify alliteration easily, use the interactive activity 'Sound patterns' beforehand.
Extension: Use self-evaluation for the children to assess the inventiveness of their word choices. Suggest comparing lists with a partner, to offer comments and evaluation on their alliterative choices.

Key aspects of learning
Communication: Children will begin to develop their ability to discuss patterns in the poetry and to create their own using carefully chosen words and phrases. They will sometimes work collaboratively in pairs and groups. They will communicate outcomes orally and in writing (possibly including ICT).

POETRY

Periodic assessment

Reading

Learning outcome
Children can listen to, read and perform poems, identifying different patterns in their language use and structure.

Success criteria
- I can identify patterns in poetry.
- I can plan and put on a poetry performance.

Setting the context
Tell the children that you are going to read them a new poem 'Questions About Slowworms' from the photocopiable page 'Poetry 1 Reading assessment text'. Before you begin, hand out a piece of paper divided into four boxes to each child. Explain that as you read the poem aloud, you will pause at the end of every four lines for them to sketch the most vivid mental image that they are left with.

Assessment opportunity
Read the text and observe the children as they make their sketches. Display the poem on the whiteboard and read it through again, encouraging the children to listen and look for patterns. Afterwards, give the children individual copies of the poem and the photocopiable page 'Poetry 1 Reading assessment (a)' to complete independently. Follow this up with the interactive activity 'Poetry 1 Reading assessment (b)' and assess children's confidence in matching the images to the words. Ask them to print off their work afterwards and then put them into pairs of comparable ability. Assign each pair half of the poem and ask them to plan a partner performance. Assess how well they work together by considering: Do they divide the speaking? Do they keep a rhythm? Do they add actions? After rehearsals, let each pair perform for an audience. Suggest pairs assess their own performance, setting themselves a target for another time.

Assessment evidence
At level 1, the children may only find one pattern and their answers may be incomplete. Their performance may be quite 'wooden' and with little body language. At levels 2–3, the children should identify two language patterns (repeated vocabulary, repeated question structure, a regular rhyme pattern) and answer all the questions. Their performance should hold an audience's attention. This activity will help you judge the children's overall understanding of work in this unit and provide evidence against Reading AF1, AF3, AF4 and AF5.

Periodic assessment

Writing

Learning outcome
Children can write a simple poem of their own, playing with interesting and inventive language choices to create or continue a particular pattern.

Success criteria
- I can continue a word pattern.
- I can play with words to create patterns in poetry.

Setting the context
Remind the children of their alliterative present lists from the Phase 3 activity 'Planning patterned poetry'. Hand back the completed lists so that the children can view them. Explain that you are going to put your list into a new, more detailed poem. On the whiteboard, start your poem:
One rushing robot to win an Olympic medal.
Two talking teddies to read out the news.

Assessment opportunity
Ask the children to look carefully at the poem and make a note of all the patterns you have used. Suggest they carry on with your poem using the presents from their own lists. Provide access to a computer or rough paper for drafts of their poems. Once they are satisfied with their draft, the children can type or write out their poem in neat. On a separate piece of paper, ask the children to describe the patterns they have tried to use and self-assess how well they have done.

Assessment evidence
Judge the children's self-assessment comments against your own assessment and act on this accordingly. Boost self-esteem where necessary by providing constructive comments and small, manageable targets. This activity will help you judge the children's overall understanding of work in this unit and provide evidence against Writing AF1, AF2 and AF7.

B, Beautiful B!

I'm a
busy, buzzing,
black and yellow bumble-bee.
Bzzz, bzzz, bzzz,
you can't catch me!

I'm a
bobbing, bouncing,
belly-dancing butterfly.
Bib, bab, bob,
watch me reach the sky!

I'm a
bossy, bungling,
bumpy-jumpy big brown bear.
Oomps-a-daisy, bumps-a-daisy,
chase me if you dare!

Judith Nicholls

Name	Date

Playing with patterns

■ Think of your own words to complete each line of the poem.

Waves

There are big, bold, _____ waves.

There are small, shy, _____ waves.

There are tidy, thoughtful, _____ waves.

There are messy, muddling, _____ waves.

There are slimy, splashing, _____ waves.

There are clear, crystal, _____ waves.

There are low, lasting, _____ waves.

There are high, hurried, _____ waves.

There are quiet, quivering, _____ waves.

There are noisy, nagging, _____ waves.

But which waves are best?

Red
Amber
Green

I can identify a word pattern. ☐

POETRY
UNIT 2 Really looking

Literacy objectives

Speak and listen for a wide range of purposes in different contexts
Strand 1 Speaking
- Speak with clarity and use appropriate intonation when reading and reciting texts.

Strand 2 Listening and responding
- Respond to presentations by describing characters, repeating some highlights and commenting constructively.

Strand 3 Group discussion and interaction
- Listen to each other's views and preferences, agree the next steps to take and identify contributions by each group member.

Strand 4 Drama
- Consider how mood and atmosphere are created in live or recorded performance.

Read and write for a range of purposes on paper and on screen
Strand 5 Word recognition: decoding (reading) and encoding (spelling)
- Read independently and with increasing fluency longer and less familiar texts.
- Spell with increasing accuracy and confidence, drawing on word recognition and knowledge of word structure, and spelling patterns.
- Know how to tackle unfamiliar words that are not completely decodable.
- Read and spell less common alternative graphemes including trigraphs.
- Read high and medium frequency words independently and automatically.

Strand 6 Word structure and spelling
- Spell with increasing accuracy and confidence, drawing on word recognition and knowledge of word structure and spelling patterns, including common inflections and use of double letters.
- Read and spell less common alternative graphemes including trigraphs.

Strand 7 Understanding and interpreting texts
- Explore how particular words are used, including words and expressions with similar meanings.

Strand 8 Engaging with and responding to texts
- Explain their reactions to texts, commenting on important aspects.

Strand 9 Creating and shaping texts
- Draw on knowledge and experience of texts in deciding and planning what and how to write.
- Make adventurous word and language choices appropriate to the style and purpose of the text.
- Select from different presentational features to suit particular writing purposes on paper and on screen.

Key aspects of learning

Enquiry
- Children will play games and ask questions about the descriptive detail they can find in poems.

Key aspects of learning (continued)

Reasoning
- Children will explain the ways in which poems show descriptive detail and how that descriptive detail could be continued.

Evaluation
- Children will discuss criteria for effective descriptive detail poems, give feedback to others and judge the effectiveness of their word and presentational choices.

Communication
- Children will begin to develop their ability to discuss descriptions in the poetry and to create their own carefully chosen words and phrases. They will sometimes work collaboratively in pairs and groups. They will communicate outcomes orally and in writing (possibly including ICT).

Assessment focuses

Reading
AF3 (deduce, infer or interpret information, events or ideas from texts).
AF5 (explain and comment on writers' use of language, including grammatical and literary features at word and sentence level).

Writing
AF1 (write imaginative, interesting and thoughtful texts).
AF2 (produce texts which are appropriate to task, reader and purpose).
AF3 (organise and present whole texts effectively, sequencing and structuring information, ideas and events).
AF7 (select appropriate and effective vocabulary).

Speaking and listening
Speaking (speak with clarity, intonation and pace).
Listening and responding (ask relevant questions; follow instructions).
Group discussion and interaction (take turns).
Drama (evaluate performances).

Resources

Phase 1 activities
Photocopiable page, 'At the End of a School Day'
Phase 2 activities
Photocopiable page, 'I'm Not Scared of the Monster'
Photocopiable page, 'Planning a performance'
Photocopiable page, 'Three stars and a wish'
Phase 3 activities
Photocopiable page, 'Making Music'
Phase 4 activities
Image, 'Snowman'
Photocopiable page, 'Set the scene'
Periodic assessment
Photocopiable page, 'Poetry 2 Reading assessment text'
Interactive activity, 'Poetry 2 Reading assessment'
Image, 'At the supermarket'
Photocopiable page, 'Poetry 2 Writing assessment'

Unit 2 ▢ Really looking

Learning outcomes	Assessment opportunity and evidence	Assessment focuses (AFs)	Success criteria
		Level 1	
Phase ① activities pages 147–149			
Seeing pictures Children can visualise scenes and comment on descriptions in poems.	• Independent and paired activity where children listen to a poem, and draw two images. • Children's discussions, written responses and drawings.	**Reading AF3** • Reasonable inference at a basic level. • Comments/questions about meaning of parts of text.	I can listen to a poem and remember what it described.
Painting pictures Children can relate a poem's details to their own experiences.	• Independent and paired activity where children draw images that evoke the end of their school day and write accompanying words and phrases. • Children's discussions, written responses and drawings.	**Writing AF7** • Mostly simple vocabulary. • Communicates meaning through repetition of key words.	I can compare a poem with my own experiences.
Describing my scenes Children can create a poem based on their own experiences.	• Independent activity where children use the pictures and words they recorded in the previous activity to write a poem. • Children's oral presentations and written poems.	**Writing AF2** Some indication of basic purpose, particular form or awareness of reader.	I can create a poem about my own experiences.
Phase ② activities pages 149–150			
What shall we do? Children can plan a performance of a poem.	• Paired and group activity where children listen to and role play a poem and then plan a group performance of it. • Children's notes.	**Writing AF3** • Some formulaic phrases indicate start/end of text. • Events/ideas sometimes in appropriate order.	• I can plan a performance of a poem. • I can perform a poem using dance and drama.
Let's perform! Children can respond to poetry through dance and drama, and evaluate their performance.	• Group activity where children use their plans to rehearse and perform their poems and then complete an evaluation sheet. • Children's completed self-evaluation.	**Writing AF2** Some indication of basic purpose, particular form or awareness of reader.	• I can evaluate a poetry performance. • I can perform a poem using dance and drama.
Phase ③ activities pages 150–151			
Effective words Children can recognise the careful selection of words.	• Independent and paired activity where children listen to a poem, identify and draw the instruments mentioned and then identify words in the text that best evoke each instrument. • Children's completed drawings and notes.	**Reading AF5** Comments on obvious features of language.	I can pick out the powerful words in a poem.

Unit 2 Really looking

Learning outcomes	Assessment opportunity and evidence	Assessment focuses (AFs)	Success criteria
		Level 1	
Phase ④ activities pages 151–152			
Looking and feeling Children can explore and record their feelings in response to direct observation.	• Independent and paired activity where children respond to an image of a snowman through drama and role play and then transfer their feelings into words and phrases on paper. • Individual role play and partner discussion. • Children's notes.	**Writing AF1** • Basic information and ideas conveyed through appropriate word choice. • Some descriptive language.	• I can use drama to explore a scene. • I can write poetry after looking closely at an object.
Sharing details Children can write a simple poem of their own in response to direct observation.	• Independent and paired activity where children write a poem about a snowman. • Individual role play. • Children's edited plans and completed poem.	**Writing AF1** • Basic information and ideas conveyed through appropriate word choice. • Some descriptive language.	I can write poetry after looking closely at an object.

Learning outcomes	Assessment opportunity and evidence	Assessment focuses (AFs)		Success criteria
		Level 2	Level 3	
Phase ① activities pages 147–149				
Seeing pictures Children can visualise scenes and comment on descriptions in poems.	• Independent and paired activity where children listen to a poem, draw two images. • Children's discussions of the poem, written responses and drawings.	**Reading AF3** • Simple, plausible inference about events and information, using evidence from text. • Comments based on textual cues, sometimes misunderstood.	**Reading AF3** • Straightforward inference based on a single point of reference in the text. • Responses to text show meaning established at a literal level or based on personal speculation.	I can listen to a poem and remember what it described.
Painting pictures Children can relate a poem's details to their own experiences.	• Independent and paired activity where children draw a series of images that evoke the end of their school day and write accompanying words and phrases. • Children's discussions, written responses and drawings.	**Writing AF7** • Simple, often speech-like vocabulary conveys relevant meanings. • Some adventurous word choices.	**Writing AF7** • Simple, generally appropriate vocabulary used, limited in range. • Some words selected for effect or occasion.	I can compare a poem with my own experiences.
Describing my scenes Children can create a poem based on their own experiences.	• Independent activity where children use the pictures and words they recorded in the previous activity to write a poem. • Children's oral presentations and written poems.	**Writing AF2** • Some basic purpose established. • Some appropriate features of the given form used. • Some attempts to adopt appropriate style.	**Writing AF2** • Purpose established at a general level. • Main features of selected form sometimes signalled to the reader. • Some attempts at appropriate style, with attention to reader.	I can create a poem about my own experiences.

POETRY

Learning outcomes	Assessment opportunity and evidence	Assessment focuses (AFs)		Success criteria
		Level 2	Level 3	
Phase ② activities pages 149-150				
What shall we do? Children can plan a performance of a poem.	● Paired and group activity where children listen to and role play a poem and then plan a group performance of it. ● Children's notes.	**Writing AF3** ● Some basic sequencing of ideas or material. ● Openings and/or closings sometimes signalled.	**Writing AF3** ● Some attempt to organise ideas with related points placed next to each other. ● Openings and closings usually signalled. ● Some attempt to sequence ideas or material logically.	● I can plan a performance of a poem. ● I can perform a poem using dance and drama.
Let's perform! Children can respond to poetry through dance and drama, and evaluate their performance.	● Group activity where children use their plans from the previous activity to rehearse and perform their poems and then complete an evaluation sheet. ● Children's completed self-evaluation.	**Writing AF2** ● Some basic purpose established. ● Some appropriate features of the given form used. ● Some attempts to adopt appropriate style.	**Writing AF2** ● Purpose established at a general level. ● Main features of selected form sometimes signalled to the reader. ● Some attempts at appropriate style, with attention to reader.	● I can evaluate a poetry performance. ● I can perform a poem using dance and drama.
Phase ③ activities pages 150-151				
Effective words Children can recognise the careful selection of words.	● Independent and paired activity where children listen to a poem, identify and draw the instruments mentioned and then identify words in the text that best evoke each instrument. ● Children's completed drawings and notes.	**Reading AF5** ● Some effective language choices noted. ● Some familiar patterns of language identified.	**Reading AF5** A few basic features of writer's use of language identified, but with little or no comment.	I can pick out the powerful words in a poem.
Phase ④ activities pages 151-152				
Looking and feeling Children can explore and record their feelings in response to direct observation.	● Independent and paired activity where children respond to an image of a snowman through drama and role play and then transfer their feelings into words and phrases on paper. ● Children's notes.	**Writing AF1** ● Mostly relevant ideas and content, sometimes repetitive or sparse. ● Some apt word choices create interest. ● Brief comments, questions about events or actions suggest viewpoint.	**Writing AF1** ● Some appropriate ideas and content included. ● Some attempt to elaborate on basic information or events. ● Attempt to adopt viewpoint, though often not maintained or inconsistent.	● I can use drama to explore a scene. ● I can write poetry after looking closely at an object.
Sharing details Children can write a simple poem of their own in response to direct observation.	● Independent and paired activity where children use their experiences from the previous activity to write a poem about a snowman. ● Individual role play, adding further notes to plan. ● Children's edited plans and completed poem.	**Writing AF1** ● Mostly relevant ideas and content, sometimes repetitive or sparse. ● Some apt word choices create interest. ● Brief comments, questions about events or actions suggest viewpoint.	**Writing AF1** ● Some appropriate ideas and content included. ● Some attempt to elaborate on basic information or events. ● Attempt to adopt viewpoint, though often not maintained or inconsistent.	I can write poetry after looking closely at an object.

Phase ① Seeing pictures

Learning outcome
Children can visualise scenes and comment on descriptions in poems.

Success criteria
I can listen to a poem and remember what it described.

Setting the context
The children should have seen and read poems with descriptive detail, focusing on experiences that they can relate to. Begin the session by telling everyone that they are going to play a listening and drawing game. Provide each child with a sheet of paper divided into two.

Assessment opportunity
Read aloud the poem 'At the End of a School Day' from the photocopiable page. Afterwards, ask the children to draw the two clearest images from the poem that they can remember. After another reading, ask them to imagine the words set out on a page. Would they look like poetry or prose? Invite the children to discuss this in pairs. Listen to partner discussion to assess recognition that description may be poetry or prose. Provide pairs with a copy of the poem. Are they surprised when they see the words on the page? Using the text, ask them to find the words that gave them their two clearest pictures and write these underneath their drawings.

Assessment evidence
At level 1, the children will visualise scenes and, with encouragement, find the words that painted them. They should recognise that poems and prose can sound similar. At levels 2-3, children should express a vivid response to words and make good contributions to discussions. This activity will provide evidence towards Reading AF3.

Next steps
Support: After the children have drawn their pictures, read the poem again slowly, asking them to highlight the text when they hear the words that gave them their pictures.
Extension: Ask the children if they can find any patterns in the poem. What can they discover about its lines and verses?

Key aspects of learning
Enquiry: Children will play games and ask questions about the descriptive detail they can find in poems.
Reasoning: Children will explain the ways in which poems show descriptive detail and how that descriptive detail could be continued.

Phase ① Painting pictures

Learning outcome
Children can relate a poem's details to their own experiences.

Success criteria
I can compare a poem with my own experiences.

Setting the context
Remind the children of the previous activity, by re-reading the poem 'At the End of a School Day' from the photocopiable page. Give them time to think about the end of their own school day and how it might compare with the poet's ideas.

Assessment opportunity
Provide the children with a sheet of paper divided into four. Ask them to draw a picture from the end of their own school day in each of the boxes. On a separate sheet of paper, invite them to jot down and experiment with descriptive words linking to the images that they have drawn. In pairs, ask the children to share and

Unit 2 ☐ Really looking

comment on each other's words, and help each other improve their descriptive phrases. Challenge those at levels 2-3 to write a descriptive line for each of their pictures. Let the children self-evaluate their writing afterwards.

Assessment evidence
At level 1, the children should be able to describe briefly what is in the poem and, with help, make a link to their own experiences. Their descriptions will be shorter and lack detail. At levels 2-3, the children's pictures will show an ability to relate a poem to their experiences. They should use words well to describe what is in a picture, listening to their partner's reactions and offering suggestions. This activity will provide evidence towards Writing AF7.

Next steps
Support: Offer support when needed by asking the children about their pictures and pointing out words in their oral answers that they could use for their sentences.
Extension: Encourage the children to extend their descriptions to two lines of writing for each picture they are trying to paint.

Key aspects of learning
Communication: Children will begin to develop their ability to discuss descriptions in the poetry and to create their own carefully chosen words and phrases. They will sometimes work collaboratively in pairs and groups. They will communicate outcomes orally and in writing (possibly including ICT).

Phase ① Describing my scenes

Learning outcome
Children can create a poem based on their own experiences.

Success criteria
I can create a poem about my own experiences.

Setting the context
Ensure the children have had experience of using the terms: 'line', 'verse' and 'rhyme' when discussing poetry structure, and have completed the previous activity. Remind them of their drawings and sentences, and hand back the children's copies for them to review. Display the poem 'At the End of a School Day'. Ask the children to comment on its structure and its lack of rhyme.

Assessment opportunity
Ask the children to use their previous descriptions to create a similar poem of four verses, with each verse describing one of the four scenes that they drew. In order to use descriptive language more effectively, suggest that they pretend they are talking to someone as they write their poem. Encourage the children to write their descriptions in lines and verses, but not to use rhyme, and to work on initial drafts before writing their final poems. Give everyone the opportunity to recite their poem to a partner or group.

Assessment evidence
At level 1, the children will need help to structure their writing as a poem. At levels 2-3, the children's descriptive language will be structured as a poem and show a clear attempt to use language to create visual pictures in the mind. This activity will provide evidence towards Writing AF2.

Next steps
Support: Suggest that the children write a poem divided into four short verses of one to two lines each.
Extension: Refer the children back to the poem 'At the End of a School Day'. Ask them to identify details that are closest to their own experiences. How do they differ?

Key aspects of learning
Evaluation: Children will discuss criteria for effective descriptive detail poems, give feedback to others and judge the effectiveness of their word and presentational choices.
Communication: Children will begin to develop their ability to discuss descriptions in the poetry and to create their own carefully chosen words and phrases. They will sometimes work collaboratively in pairs and groups. They will communicate outcomes orally and in writing (possibly including ICT).

Phase ② What shall we do?

Learning outcome
Children can plan a performance of a poem.

Success criteria
● I can plan a performance of a poem.
● I can perform a poem using dance and drama.

Setting the context
Ensure the children have had experience of responding to a poem with actions as well as following a poem's rhythm and keeping time. Read aloud the poem 'I'm Not Scared of the Monster' from the photocopiable page. Discuss what happens in the poem as a whole class.

Assessment opportunity
Put the children into pairs and invite them to choose roles – one playing the monster and the other taking on the role of the child. Watch as the children act and stay in role when the poem is read aloud again. Put pairs together into groups of four and ask them to plan and discuss a group performance of the poem. Prompt them to consider how they will divide up the poem and ensure that everyone has a role, as well as thinking about the movements and facial expressions that they will use. Give everyone the photocopiable page 'Planning a performance' to record their decisions. Encourage use of notes and diagrams so the children will remember what their plans mean. Ask them to explain their plans.

Assessment evidence
At level 1, the children will have some ideas to offer the group. At levels 2-3, the children should offer a greater number of more imaginative ideas and interact well in a group. This activity will provide evidence towards Writing AF3.

Next steps
Support: Help the children to make a simple audio recording of what they want to do, or a recording of what they say they plan to do.
Extension: Encourage the children to scrutinise the words of the poem, checking that they have actions for every part, and to consider if sound effects would help.

Key aspects of learning
Evaluation: Children will discuss criteria for effective descriptive detail poems, give feedback to others and judge the effectiveness of their word and presentational choices.
Communication: Children will begin to develop their ability to discuss descriptions in the poetry and to create their own carefully chosen words and phrases. They will sometimes work collaboratively in pairs and groups. They will communicate outcomes orally and in writing (possibly including ICT).

POETRY

Phase ② Let's perform!

Learning outcome
Children can respond to poetry through dance and drama, and evaluate their performance.

Success criteria
● I can evaluate a poetry performance.
● I can perform a poem using dance and drama.

Setting the context
Remind the children of their performance plans from the previous activity. Provide everyone with a copy of the poem 'I'm Not Scared of the Monster' from the photocopiable page and read it together.

Assessment opportunity
Put the children into the same groups as before. Allow time for groups to rehearse their performances of the poem 'I'm Not Scared of the Monster', using the notes that they wrote from the previous session as a guide. Then, invite each group to present their performance to the rest of the class, while everyone recites the poem together. Afterwards, give everyone the photocopiable page 'Three stars and a wish' to evaluate their performance.

Assessment evidence
At level 1, the children will demonstrate that they are aware of the rhythm and the message of the poem. Group work will be limited, but they will attempt to convey meaning through body language. At levels 2-3, the children will show appreciation of the rhythm and the message of the poem. They will collaborate with their group and attempt to convey meaning through body language. This activity will provide evidence towards Writing AF2.

Next steps
Support: Help the children to interpret their notes and plans into a coherent performance.
Extension: Challenge the children to write performance instructions for someone else.

Key aspects of learning
Evaluation: Children will discuss criteria for effective descriptive detail poems, give feedback to others and judge the effectiveness of their word and presentational choices.

Phase ③ Effective words

Learning outcome
Children can recognise the careful selection of words.

Success criteria
I can pick out the powerful words in a poem.

Setting the context
Explain to the children that they will be listening to a poem with descriptive detail. The poem is about musical instruments and the children will draw the instruments in the order they are mentioned. There may be other details that the poet supplies that will make their pictures more detailed.

Assessment opportunity
Provide everyone with a sheet of paper, divided into five numbered boxes. Read the poem 'Making Music' from the photocopiable page, providing the children with ample time to draw each verse's musical instrument in the appropriate box on their sheet. Afterwards, look at the words of the poem together. In pairs, ask the children to compare their pictures to check if their order is correct. Using the poem

■SCHOLASTIC

for reference, ask them to identify the descriptive word or words from each verse that they think best describes each instrument. Ask them to write these underneath their drawings, justifying orally or in writing the choices that they have made.

Assessment evidence

At level 1, the children's explanations for their word choices will be oral. At levels 2–3, the children will be able to discuss and then write their reasons. This activity will provide evidence towards Reading AF5.

Next steps

Support: For the children with poor listening skills, concentrate on just two or three verses from the poem.
Extension: Ask the children to suggest additional words for each verse that will effectively describe the sound of that musical instrument.

Key aspects of learning

Enquiry: Children will play games and ask questions about the descriptive detail they can find in poems.
Reasoning: Children will explain the ways in which poems show descriptive detail and how that descriptive detail could be continued.

Phase ④ Looking and feeling

Learning outcome
Children can explore and record their feelings in response to direct observation.

Success criteria
● I can use drama to explore a scene.
● I can write poetry after looking closely at an object.

Setting the context

Talk about occasions when it has snowed and share experiences of playing in the snow and making or seeing a snowman. Show the children the image 'Snowman' from the CD-ROM. Invite volunteers to describe what they can see in the image.

Assessment opportunity

Hold a drama session, asking the children to imagine that they are building the snowman. Talk them through the various stages, from rolling the snow and adding features, to looking at and admiring their snowman when he is complete. Then ask the children to imagine that he is starting to melt away. Encourage them to respond accordingly. Repeat the activity, this time asking the children to share their feelings at each of the three stages (building, admiring, melting away) with a talk partner. Invite them to fill in the photocopiable page 'Set the scene' using the words and phrases they have discussed.

Assessment evidence

At level 1, the children will have expressed some details about the snowman and their own feelings about him. There will be limited evidence that they empathised and used words to express this. At levels 2–3, the children will demonstrate empathy with the builder of the snowman or the snowman himself and will have made some thoughtful choices of vocabulary to express this. This activity will provide evidence towards Writing AF1.

Next steps

Support: Use questions to prompt the children's notes. For example: *How do you feel when you are building the snowman? What do his eyes look like? Does he seem proud or sad?*
Extension: Suggest the children read their completed photocopiable to a partner to hear feedback on the effectiveness of their choice of words.

POETRY

Key aspects of learning
Evaluation: Children will discuss criteria for effective descriptive detail poems, give feedback to others and judge the effectiveness of their word and presentational choices.
Communication: Children will begin to develop their ability to discuss descriptions in the poetry and to create their own carefully chosen words and phrases. They will sometimes work collaboratively in pairs and groups. They will communicate outcomes orally and in writing (possibly including ICT).

Phase ④ Sharing details

Learning outcome
Children can write a simple poem of their own in response to direct observation.

Success criteria
I can write poetry after looking closely at an object.

Setting the context
Remind the children of their work from the previous activity. Hand back the notes that they wrote on the photocopiable page 'Set the scene'.

Assessment opportunity
View the image 'Snowman' from the CD-ROM and repeat the previous drama activity. During the drama, encourage the children to add further words and notes to their photocopiable if they want to. Afterwards, ask the children to extend their words into a three-part poem, perhaps using these starters:
As I build my snowman…
The finished snowman…
As he melts away…
Encourage drafts, ideally on computer so that changes and improvements are easier to make. Suggest the children occasionally try out their lines by reading them aloud to a partner. Finish the session with poetry readings – the audience sitting with their eyes closed as a poem's words work their magic.

Assessment evidence
At level 1, the children may write short verses of only one to two lines and their organisation may be poor and unstructured. At levels 2–3, the children will demonstrate that they can organise their thoughts and will have selected some words with care. This activity will provide evidence towards Writing AF1.

Next steps
Support: Supply the children with a writing frame, with the suggested starters from above starting their three verses.
Extension: To improve evaluation skills, ask partners to read their poems aloud to each other. Encourage them to discuss their reactions. Do the snowmen seem real?

Key aspects of learning
Communication: Children will begin to develop their ability to discuss descriptions in the poetry and to create their own carefully chosen words and phrases. They will sometimes work collaboratively in pairs and groups. They will communicate outcomes orally and in writing (possibly including ICT).

Periodic assessment

Reading

Learning outcome
Children can recognise the careful selection of words.

Success criteria
- I can recognise why poets choose the words they do.
- I can pick out the powerful words in a poem.

Setting the context
Tell the children that they are going to read a poem and think about how the poet uses descriptions. Give them each a copy of the poem 'Drum' on the photocopiable page 'Poetry 2 Reading assessment text' and read it aloud.

Assessment opportunity
Ask the children to work independently, using the poem to help them complete the interactive activity 'Poetry 2 Reading assessment'. Observe the attention the children give to reading the text, and assess their confidence in selecting words to highlight. Observe as partners prepare and then read and perform the poem.

Assessment evidence
At level 1, the children may fail to identify the correct words and will need reminding to re-read the poem. At levels 2–3, the children should identify words more competently. This activity will help you judge the children's overall understanding of work in this unit and provide evidence against Reading AF1, AF2, AF3.

POETRY

Periodic assessment

Writing

Learning outcome
Children can write a simple poem of their own in response to direct observation.

Success criteria
● I can write poetry after looking closely at an object.
● I can create a poem about my own experiences.

Setting the context
Ask the children to picture in their mind a recent shopping trip. Display the image 'At the supermarket' from the CD-ROM. Ask the children to describe what they can see in the image, prompting them by asking questions: *What is happening in the picture? Is this what you do? What would you be thinking? Does the fruit look mouth-watering? What makes you feel hungry?*

Assessment opportunity
Ask the children to paint the scene as a poem. Suggest noting words and phrases they may want to use before deciding on a structure and drafting their poem. Provide children with the photocopiable page, 'Poetry 2 Writing assessment' to record a neat copy of their poem. Afterwards, put the children into pairs to read their poems to each other, encouraging the listeners to describe their responses to the poem: *What do they see? What do they feel?* The children can then perform their own self-assessment of their poem.

Assessment evidence
Judge the children's self-assessment comments against your own assessment and act accordingly. Boost self-esteem where necessary by commenting on particularly interesting and evocative words and set a manageable target for the next poem. This activity will help you judge the children's overall understanding of work in this unit and provide evidence against Writing AF1, AF2 and AF7.

POETRY

At the End of a School Day

It is the end of a school day

    and down the long drive

come bag-swinging, shouting children.

    Deafened, the sky winces.

        The sun gapes in surprise.

Suddenly the runners skid to a stop,

    stand still and stare

at a small hedgehog

    curled-up on the tarmac

        like an old, frayed cricket ball.

A girl dumps her bag, tiptoes forward

    and gingerly, so gingerly

carries the creature

    to the safety of a shady hedge.

        Then steps back, watching.

Girl, children, sky and sun

    hold their breath.

There is a silence,

    a moment to remember

        on this warm afternoon in June.

Wes Magee

Name   Date

Three stars and a wish

These children were in my group: _____

_____

I was pleased with my part in our performance for these three reasons:

★ _____

_____

★ _____

_____

★ _____

_____

Next time I perform a poem, I will try to make this improvement:

_____

_____

_____

_____

_____

_____

Red
Amber   I can evaluate a poetry performance. ▢
Green

POETRY

Making Music

I'm a BIG BASS drum
booming down the street,
tapping with my fingers
to the booming bass beat.

I'm a fiddle playing music
shooting notes up high,
watching as they fall
from a music-making sky.

I'm an old double bass
grumbling in my boots,
shaking every tree top
down to its roots.

I'm a small brass horn
singing to the stars,
swimming in their moonshine
and diving down to Mars.

I'm a cymbal sitting still
making not a sound,
waiting for the moment
when I CRASH to the ground.

Andrew Collett

POETRY
UNIT 3 Silly stuff

Literacy objectives

Speak and listen for a wide range of purposes in different contexts
Strand 1 Speaking
- Speak with clarity and use appropriate intonation when reading and reciting texts.

Strand 2 Listening and responding
- Respond to presentations by describing characters, repeating some highlights and commenting constructively.

Strand 3 Group discussion and interaction
- Listen to each other's views and preferences, agree the next steps to take and identify contributions by each group member.

Strand 4 Drama
- Consider how mood and atmosphere are created in live or recorded performance.

Read and write for a range of purposes on paper and on screen
Strand 5 Word recognition: decoding (reading) and encoding (spelling)
- Read independently and with increasing fluency longer and less familiar texts.
- Spell with increasing accuracy and confidence, drawing on word recognition and knowledge of word structure, and spelling patterns.
- Know how to tackle unfamiliar words that are not completely decodable.
- Read and spell less common alternative graphemes including trigraphs.
- Read high and medium frequency words independently and automatically.

Strand 6 Word structure and spelling
- Spell with increasing accuracy and confidence, drawing on word recognition and knowledge of word structure, and spelling patterns including common inflections and use of double letters.
- Read and spell less common alternative graphemes including trigraphs.

Strand 7 Understanding and interpreting texts
- Explore how particular words are used, including words and expressions with similar meanings.

Strand 8 Engaging with and responding to texts
- Explain their reactions to texts, commenting on important aspects.

Strand 9 Creating and shaping texts
- Draw on knowledge and experience of texts in deciding and planning what and how to write.
- Make adventurous word and language choices appropriate to the style and purpose of the text.
- Select from different presentational features to suit particular writing purposes on paper and on screen.

Key aspects of learning

Enquiry
- Children will play games and assess how funny language can be in poems.

Reasoning
- Children will explain the ways in which language is humorous.

Key aspects of learning (continued)

Evaluation
● Children will find ways to use language playfully, give feedback to others and judge the effectiveness of their word and presentational choices.
Communication
● Children will begin to develop their ability to discuss word play in the poetry and to create their own using carefully chosen words and phrases. They will sometimes work collaboratively in pairs and groups. They will communicate outcomes orally and in writing (possibly including ICT).

Assessment focuses

Reading
AF5 (explain and comment on writers' use of language, including grammatical and literary features at word and sentence level).
AF6 (identify and comment on writers' purposes and viewpoints, and the overall effect of the text on the reader).

Writing
AF1 (write imaginative, interesting and thoughtful texts).
AF2 (produce texts which are appropriate to task, reader and purpose).
AF7 (select appropriate and effective vocabulary).

Speaking and listening
Speaking (speak with clarity and use intonation when reading and reciting texts).
Listening and responding (listen to others in class).
Group discussion and interaction (make contributions to sustain the activity).
Drama (evaluate performances).

Resources

Phase 1 activities
Photocopiable page, 'Eletelephony'
Photocopiable page, 'Betty Botter'
Interactive activity, 'Identifying alliteration'
Photocopiable page, 'Tongue-twisters'
Phase 2 activities
Photocopiable page, 'Jabberwocky'
Photocopiable page, 'The Pobble Who Has No Toes'
Interactive activity, 'Jabberwocky'
Phase 3 activities
Photocopiable page, 'Inventing humour'
Phase 4 activities
Photocopiable page, 'Three Wicked Witchesses'
Photocopiable page, 'Why is it funny?'
Periodic assessment
Photocopiable page, 'Poetry 3 Reading assessment text'
Interactive activity, 'Poetry 3 Reading assessment'
Photocopiable page, 'Poetry 3 Writing assessment'

Unit 3 ◻ Silly stuff

Learning outcomes	Assessment opportunity and evidence	Assessment focuses (AFs)	Success criteria
		Level 1	
Phase ① activities pages 163-164			
Being funny Children can recognise lines with humorous language.	• Paired activity where children respond to a humorous poem using facial expressions and then read the text and identify the funny words. • Children's notes.	**Reading AF6** Some simple comments about preferences, mostly linked to own experience.	I can say what makes a poem seem funny.
Sounds silly Children can recognise and create lines with humorous language.	• Independent and paired activity where children listen to a tongue-twister, vote whether it is 'serious' or 'silly' and explore alliterative words and phrases. • Children's completed interactive activity and photocopiable.	**Writing AF7** • Mostly simple vocabulary. • Communicates meaning through repetition of key words.	• I can identify funny words in a poem. • I can create a funny poem using words that start with the same sound.
Phase ② activities pages 164-165			
Responding to words Children can listen to and respond to poems.	• Independent and paired activity where children listen to the poem 'Jabberwocky' and record in pictures and words what they visualise during the reading. • Children's pictures and written notes.	**Writing AF2** Some indication of basic purpose, particular form or awareness of reader.	• I can respond to poems through pictures. • I can identify funny words in a poem.
Using strange words Children can listen to, respond to and perform poems.	• Independent and group activity where children identify the nonsense words in the poem 'Jabberwocky' by completing an interactive activity and then plan a drama performance of the poem. • Children's group performances.	**Reading AF6** Some simple comments about preferences, mostly linked to own experience.	I can respond to poems through drama.
Phase ③ activities pages 165-166			
Inventing humour Children can write a humorous poem of their own.	• Paired activity where children add additional humorous lines to the poem 'In The Flin Flun Flon'. • Children's completed poem on the photocopiable.	**Writing AF1** • Basic information and ideas conveyed through appropriate word choice. • Some descriptive language.	I can create a funny poem.

Unit 3 📗 Silly stuff

Learning outcomes	Assessment opportunity and evidence	Assessment focuses (AFs)	Success criteria
		Level 1	
Phase ④ activities pages 166-167			
Why is it funny? Children can recognise lines in a poem with humorous language and respond to it using dance and drama.	• Independent and paired activity where children read the poem 'Three Wicked Witchesses', identify the humorous words and then devise actions for the poem. • Children's written responses on the photocopiable.	**Reading AF5** Comments on obvious features of language.	• I can identify funny words in a poem. • I can perform a poem using drama and dance.
Writing silly stuff Children can write a simple poem of their own, playing with interesting and inventive language choices to create or continue a particular pattern.	• Paired activity where children use the poem 'Three Wicked Witchesses' as a template to plan and write their own poem about three princesses. • Children's completed poems.	**Writing AF7** • Mostly simple vocabulary. • Communicates meaning through repetition of key words.	• I can use words and patterns to create a funny poem. • I can evaluate my poetry writing.

Learning outcomes	Assessment opportunity and evidence	Assessment focuses (AFs)		Success criteria
		Level 2	Level 3	
Phase ① activities pages 163-164				
Being funny Children can recognise lines with humorous language.	• Paired activity where children respond to a humorous poem using facial expressions and then read the text and identify the funny words. • Children's written notes.	**Reading AF6** • Some awareness that writers have viewpoints and purposes. • Simple statements about likes and dislikes in reading, sometimes with reasons.	**Reading AF6** • Comments identify main purpose. • Express personal response but with little awareness of writer's viewpoint or effect on reader.	I can say what makes a poem seem funny.
Sounds silly Children can recognise and create lines with humorous language.	• Independent and paired activity where children listen to a tongue-twister, vote whether it is 'serious' or 'silly' and explore alliterative words and phrases. • Children's completed interactive activity and photocopiable.	**Writing AF7** • Simple, often speech-like vocabulary conveys relevant meanings. • Some adventurous word choices.	**Writing AF7** • Simple, generally appropriate vocabulary used, limited in range. • Some words selected for effect or occasion.	• I can identify funny words in a poem. • I can create a funny poem using words that start with the same sound.

Unit 3 ◫ Silly stuff

Learning outcomes	Assessment opportunity and evidence	Assessment focuses (AFs)		Success criteria
		Level 2	Level 3	
Phase ② activities pages 164-165				
Responding to words Children can listen to and respond to poems.	• Independent and paired activity where children listen to the poem 'Jabberwocky' and record in pictures and words what they visualise during the reading. • Children's pictures and written notes.	**Writing AF2** • Some basic purpose established. • Some appropriate features of the given form used. • Some attempts to adopt appropriate style.	**Writing AF2** • Purpose established at a general level. • Main features of selected form sometimes signalled to the reader. • Some attempts at appropriate style, with attention to reader.	• I can respond to poems through pictures. • I can identify funny words in a poem.
Using strange words Children can listen to, respond to and perform poems.	• Independent and group activity where children identify the nonsense words in the poem 'Jabberwocky' by completing an interactive activity and then plan a drama performance of the poem. • Children's group performances.	**Reading AF6** • Some awareness that writers have viewpoints and purposes. • Simple statements about likes and dislikes in reading, sometimes with reasons.	**Reading AF6** • Comments identify main purpose. • Express personal response but with little awareness of writer's viewpoint or effect on reader.	I can respond to poems through drama.
Phase ③ activities pages 165-166				
Inventing humour Children can write a humorous poem of their own.	• Paired activity where children add additional humorous lines to the poem 'In The Flin Flun Flon'. • Paired discussion of the poem and their ideas. • Children's completed poem on the photocopiable.	**Writing AF1** • Mostly relevant ideas and content, sometimes repetitive or sparse. • Some apt word choices create interest. • Brief comments, questions about events or actions suggest viewpoint.	**Writing AF1** • Some appropriate ideas and content included. • Some attempt to elaborate on basic information or events. • Attempt to adopt viewpoint, though often not maintained or inconsistent.	I can create a funny poem.
Phase ④ activities pages 166-167				
Why is it funny? Children can recognise lines in a poem with humorous language and respond to it using dance and drama.	• Independent and paired activity where children read the poem 'Three Wicked Witchesses', identify the humorous words and then devise actions for the poem. • Children's written responses on the photocopiable.	**Reading AF5** • Some effective language choices noted. • Some familiar patterns of language identified.	**Reading AF5** A few basic features of writer's use of language identified, but with little or no comment.	• I can identify funny words in a poem. • I can perform a poem using drama and dance.
Writing silly stuff Children can write a simple poem of their own, playing with interesting and inventive language choices to create or continue a particular pattern.	• Independent and paired activity where children use the poem 'Three Wicked Witchesses' as a template to plan and write their own poem about three princesses. • Children's completed poems.	**Writing AF7** • Simple, often speech-like vocabulary conveys relevant meanings. • Some adventurous word choices.	**Writing AF7** • Simple, generally appropriate vocabulary used, limited in range. • Some words selected for effect or occasion.	• I can use words and patterns to create a funny poem. • I can evaluate my poetry writing.

Phase ① Being funny

Success criteria
I can say what makes a poem seem funny.

Setting the context
Ensure the children have had experience of listening to poems and discussing them with others.

Assessment opportunity
Read the poem 'Eletelephony' from the photocopiable page, encouraging the children to show their reactions to the text using facial expressions. Give partners the text to look at together. Ask them to read out parts to each other so that they can identify the words that make them laugh. Ask them to write down those words and explain to their partner why they find them funny and what they notice about their sounds. Can the children list some proper words that get confused with one another in the poem? What nonsense words do they become?

Assessment evidence
At level 1, the children will recognise that some words sound silly and the poem does not really make sense. At levels 2–3, the children should realise that some words are invented, based on a confusion of the sounds in the other words. This activity will provide evidence towards Reading AF6.

Next steps
Support: Work with a group of children and use only verse 1 of the poem. Record their oral comments.
Extension: Challenge the children to add a verse about the elephant's tail to the poem.

Key aspects of learning
Enquiry: Children will play games and assess how funny language can be in poems.
Reasoning: Children will explain the ways in which language is humorous.

Phase ① Sounds silly

Success criteria
● I can identify funny words in a poem.
● I can create a funny poem using words that start with the same sound.

Setting the context
Prior to this assessment, ensure the children have had experience of alliteration and tongue-twisters. Tell them you are going to read a poem aloud and they are going to give their opinion by holding up a voting board. Provide everyone with 'silly' and 'serious' cards.

Assessment opportunity
Read the children the poem 'Betty Botter' from the photocopiable page, and ask them to vote whether they think it is a silly or a serious poem. Invite them to tell a partner why they voted as they did. Give children the interactive activity 'Identifying alliteration'. Read the instructions together but let the children highlight the words independently. Afterwards, give them the photocopiable page 'Tongue-twisters' to complete.

Assessment evidence

At level 1, the children will have shown some grasp of alliteration. Their tongue-twisters are likely to be short and need support. At levels 2-3, the children will show a definite grasp of alliteration and demonstrate some ability to be inventive with language. This activity will provide evidence towards Writing AF7.

Next steps

Support: Suggest the children add only two more words to make their tongue-twister.
Extension: Encourage the children to introduce a new character to their own tongue-twister.

Key aspects of learning

Communication: Children will begin to develop their ability to discuss word play in the poetry and to create their own using carefully chosen words and phrases. They will sometimes work collaboratively in pairs and groups. They will communicate outcomes orally and in writing (possibly including ICT).

Phase ② Responding to words

Learning outcome

Children can listen to and respond to poems.

Success criteria

- I can respond to poems through pictures.
- I can identify funny words in a poem.

Setting the context

Ensure the children have had experience of listening to unseen texts and describing images the words put into their minds. Read aloud the poem 'Jabberwocky' from the unseen photocopiable page. Ask the children to share reactions with a partner, as you prompt their discussion with questions: *Did you find the poem funny? Why? Which words?*

Assessment opportunity

Read the poem aloud a second time, inviting the children to close their eyes in order for the poem's words to form a picture of the Jabberwocky in their minds. Let the children put that picture onto paper and write under the picture the words or detail in the poem that helped them decide what to draw.

Assessment evidence

At level 1, the children's work will be mainly drawn and oral. They will need help in identifying a few relevant words in the poem. At levels 2-3, the children will show care in their choice of vocabulary in order to express their feelings about the poem to their partner and will produce a text that conveys their response. The activity will provide evidence towards Writing AF2.

Next steps

Support: If the children find the poem too difficult, use the photocopiable page 'The Pobble Who Has No Toes'.
Extension: Ask the children to explain their pictures to each other in a small group. Emphasise that there cannot be a wrong picture as the poet leaves the reader to form their own pictures and opinions.

Key aspects of learning

Reasoning: Children will explain the ways in which language is humorous.
Communication: Children will begin to develop their ability to discuss word play in the poetry and to create their own using carefully chosen words and phrases. They will sometimes work collaboratively in pairs and groups. They will communicate outcomes orally and in writing (possibly including ICT).

Phase ② Using strange words

Learning outcome
Children can listen to, respond to and perform poems.

Success criteria
I can respond to poems through drama.

Setting the context
Ensure the children have had experience of responding to a poem with actions as well as following a poem's rhythm and keeping time. Give the children a copy of the photocopiable 'Jabberwocky' from the previous activity and read it aloud with them. Discuss what happens in the poem.

Assessment opportunity
Assess the children's understanding that words may be nonsense by giving them the interactive activity 'Jabberwocky' to complete. Afterwards, re-read the poem and then put the children into small groups to discuss what happens. Suggest that the groups show their interpretation in action and mime. Let each group perform to the class ('audience'), while the audience recites the poem.

Assessment evidence
At level 1, the children would benefit from carrying out the interactive activity with a partner of comparable ability. At levels 2-3, the children will be able to work independently on the interactive activity. This activity will provide evidence towards Reading AF6.

Next steps
Support: Help the children to read the interactive activity.
Extension: Encourage the children to scrutinise the words of the poem, stressing the importance of facial expression and body language.

Key aspects of learning
Enquiry: Children will play games and assess how funny language can be in poems.
Reasoning: Children will explain the ways in which language is humorous.

Phase ③ Inventing humour

Learning outcome
Children can write a humorous poem of their own.

Success criteria
I can create a funny poem.

Setting the context
Ensure the children are familiar with the ways in which a poem can convey humour. In particular, the use of interesting or unexpected words, alliteration and inventive language. Display and read aloud the opening verse from the poem 'In The Flin Flun Flon' from the photocopiable page 'Inventing humour'.

Assessment opportunity
Put the children into pairs of comparable ability and challenge them to add other animals to the fantasy land of Flin Flun Flon, inventing funny eating and drinking habits for their new creations. Suggest partners discuss and try out ideas in rough, saying lines aloud to each other. They should consider if their lines need alliteration or more surprising or adventurous vocabulary to make them funnier. Give everyone the photocopiable page 'Inventing humour' to complete.

Assessment evidence
At level 1, the children will rely on oral questions and suggestions to help them express their thoughts. At levels 2-3, the children will be able to demonstrate their

POETRY

ability to work with others, to follow a style already begun by a poet and to play with language to create humour. This activity will provide evidence towards Writing AF1.

Next steps
Support: Support the children by suggesting some animals to add to the poem. The children could make an oral recording of the lines they create, to be listened to and written up afterwards.
Extension: Challenge the children to write another poem about the funny things the animals do.

Key aspects of learning
Communication: Children will begin to develop their ability to discuss word play in the poetry and to create their own using carefully chosen words and phrases. They will sometimes work collaboratively in pairs and groups. They will communicate outcomes orally and in writing (possibly including ICT).

Phase ④ Why is it funny?

Learning outcome
Children can recognise lines in a poem with humorous language and respond to it using dance and drama.

Success criteria
- I can identify funny words in a poem.
- I can perform a poem using drama and dance.

Setting the context
Ensure the children have had experience of commenting orally and in writing on a poem, identifying its humorous language. Read the poem 'Three Wicked Witchesses' from the photocopiable page.

Assessment opportunity
Give the children a copy of the poem and the photocopiable page 'Why is it funny?'. Ask them to read the poem again in order to explore the language and decide what makes the poem funny for them, recording their findings on the photocopiable page. Afterwards, put the children into pairs to compare laughter ratings. Recite the poem as a class, choosing different partners to perform the actions as you reach a line.

Assessment evidence
At level 1, the children are likely to need the assessment read to them, but should recognise some understanding of the poem and awareness of its humour. At levels 2–3, the activity will demonstrate the children's understanding of the poem and its humour, and their recognition that words may be used just because of the way they sound. This activity will provide evidence towards Reading AF5.

Next steps
Support: Accept oral explanations for the children's word selections. Record them on the photocopiable page for assessment evidence.
Extension: Ask the children to hold a group discussion about the poem, telling one another why they found it humorous.

Key aspects of learning
Reasoning: Children will explain the ways in which language is humorous.

Phase ④ Writing silly stuff

Learning outcome
Children can write a simple poem of their own, playing with interesting and inventive language choices to create or continue a particular pattern.

Success criteria
- I can use words and patterns to create a funny poem.
- I can evaluate my poetry writing.

Setting the context
Display and re-read the poem 'Three Wicked Witchesses' from the photocopiable page, reminding the children of the work they did in the previous activity. Discuss the alliterative humour, silly choices of vocabulary and invented words.

Assessment opportunity
Explain that you want the children to write a similar, humorous poem called 'Three Pretty Princesses', about three princesses in a panic to get ready for the ball. Let the children brainstorm ideas and vocabulary with a partner before making a draft. Encourage them to experiment with words and lines before writing out their final version. Ask the children to recite their poem to a group.

Assessment evidence
At level 1, you may need to supply the children with a bank of words with common sounds to choose from. They may prefer to work with a partner. At levels 2–3, the children will be able to write independently. Use the activity as evidence towards Writing AF7.

Next steps
Support: Use the starting word of each line of the model poem 'Three Wicked Witchesses' as a writing frame.
Extension: Pair the children so they can listen to each other's poems, do a peer-evaluation and award a laughter score.

Key aspects of learning
Communication: Children will begin to develop their ability to discuss word play in the poetry and to create their own using carefully chosen words and phrases. They will sometimes work collaboratively in pairs and groups. They will communicate outcomes orally and in writing (possibly including ICT).

POETRY

Periodic assessment

Reading

Learning outcome	**Success criteria**

Learning outcome
Children can recognise how language choices can make a poem seem funny.

Success criteria
- I can say what makes a poem seem funny.
- I can identify funny words in a poem.

Setting the context
Tell the children that you are going to read them a poem and they are going to give their opinion by holding up a voting board. Provide everyone with 'silly' and 'serious' cards.

Assessment opportunity
Read aloud the poem '"Quack!" Said the Billy-goat' from the photocopiable page 'Poetry 3 Reading assessment text'. Afterwards, ask the children to show their response to the poem by holding up their 'serious' or 'silly' card. Give the children a copy of the poem to consult and the interactive activity 'Poetry 3 Reading assessment' to complete. This will assess the children's understanding of why the poem is funny.

Assessment evidence
At level 1, the children may need help in locating particular animals in the poem. At levels 2–3, the children should match words and pictures more quickly. This activity will help you judge the children's overall understanding of work in this unit and provide evidence against Reading AF3, AF5 and AF6.

SCHOLASTIC

Periodic assessment

Writing

Learning outcome
Children can write a simple poem of their own, playing with interesting and inventive language choices to create or continue a particular pattern.

Success criteria
- I can identify funny words in a poem.
- I can create a funny poem.
- I can evaluate my poetry writing.

Setting the context
Ensure that the children have completed the Periodic Reading assessment. Recite together the poem, '"Quack!" Said the Billy-goat' from the photocopiable page 'Poetry 3 Reading assessment text'. Agree and list on the whiteboard the animals mentioned.

Assessment opportunity
Suggest that the farm may be having some surprising new animals. For example, a lion. Ask the children to decide on four new animal arrivals and put them and their noises into a humorous poem. Suggest they note in rough their chosen four animals and their noises, before compiling their ideas into a rough draft. Afterwards, put the children into pairs to read their poem to a partner. Listeners should comment on the lines that they find the funniest. The children can use this reaction to help them decide how to complete their self-assessment using the photocopiable page 'Poetry 3 Writing assessment'.

Assessment evidence
Judge the children's self-assessment comments against your own assessment and act accordingly. Boost self-esteem where necessary by commenting on lines that made you smile and set a manageable target for the next poem. This activity will help you judge the children's overall understanding of work in this unit and provide evidence against Writing AF2 and AF7.

Eletelephony

Once there was an elephant,
Who tried to use the telephant –
No! No! I mean an elephone
Who tried to use the telephone –
(Dear me! I am not certain quite
That even now I've got it right.)

Howe'er it was, he got his trunk
Entangled in the telephunk;
The more he tried to get it free,
The louder buzzed the telephee –
(I fear I'd better drop the song
Of elephop and telephong!)

Laura E Richards

Name   Date

Tongue-twisters

◼ Write a word that begins with the same sound in front of each name. (For example: *Jolly Johnny*.)

◼ Then, write a silly tongue-twister about one or two of these people. Do it in rough first.

Johnny

Hiba

Polly

Brian

Carl

Sam

Cathy

Sabina

Tony

Red
Amber
Green

I can create a funny poem using words that start with the same sound.

POETRY

Name   Date

Why is it funny?

◼ Read the poem from the photocopiable page
'Three Wicked Witchesses'.

◼ Underline four words from the poem that you find funny.

◼ Why do you think the words are funny?

_____

_____

_____

_____

◼ Read the poem aloud to yourself and give it a laughter rating between
1 and 10. (10 being the best!)

| 1 | 2 | 3 | 4 | 5 | 6 | 7 | 8 | 9 | 10 |

Red
Amber   I can identify funny words in a poem. ☐
Green

Poetry 3 Reading assessment text

"Quack!" Said the Billy-goat

"Quack!" said the billy-goat.
"Oink!" said the hen.
"Miaow!" said the little chick
Running in the pen.

"Hobble-gobble!" said the dog.
"Cluck!" said the sow.
"Tu-whit tu-whoo!" the donkey said.
"Baa!" said the cow.

"Hee-haw!" the turkey cried.
The duck began to moo.
All at once the sheep went,
"Cock-a-doodle-doo!"

The owl coughed and cleared his throat
And he began to bleat
"Bow-wow!" said the cock
Swimming in the leat.

"Cheep-cheep!" said the cat
As she began to fly.
"Farmer's been and laid an egg –
That's the reason why."

Charles Causley

📖**SCHOLASTIC** **PHOTOCOPIABLE**

POETRY

🔲 Transitional assessment

Activity	Type	Level	Description
1.1	Reading comprehension	1	No time limit; two-part test based on non-fiction information text about animals and a narrative extract from *Duck in the Truck* by Jez Alborough
1.1	Shorter writing task	1	15 minutes; writing a recount about a favourite place you have visited
1.1	Longer writing task	1	25 minutes; writing a story about five little ducks that become lost (based on the traditional rhyme 'Five Little Ducks')
2.1	Reading comprehension	2	30-minute two-part test based on a narrative extract from *The Snow Lambs* by Debbie Gliori and the poem 'Weather at Work' by Jenny Morris
2.1	Shorter writing task	2	15 minutes; writing a report about different kinds of weather
2.1	Longer writing task	2	30 minutes; writing a recount based on personal experience of problem weather
3.1	Reading comprehension	3	30-minute two-part test based on narrative extracts from *The Sheep Pig* by Dick King-Smith and a non-fiction leaflet for a farm visitors' centre
3.1	Shorter writing task	3	15 minutes; writing an imaginative description of a special pet
3.1	Longer writing task	3	30 minutes; writing letter to persuade the teacher to take the class on a trip to a farm

NB There are two transitional assessments provided for each level. Transitional tests and tasks 1.2, 2.2 and 3.2 are not shown here. All tests and tasks are available on the CD-ROM.

Reading tests: instructions

There are two reading comprehension tests provided at each level (levels 1–3) on the CD-ROM. Each reading test is divided into two parts.

Administering the test
- There is no time limit for both parts of the test at level 1.
  - Photocopy the two short texts for each child.
  - Children should read aloud the texts with adult support only given when a child has clearly used all the reading strategies that they know.
  - After their reading of a text, ask the child the appropriate questions.
  - Children should answer questions orally.
- Allow 30 minutes for both parts of the test at levels 2 and 3.
  - Children should work unaided: do not read questions or words to them.

Equipment for each child:
- Pencil, eraser (or children may cross out mistakes).

Marking and levelling the children
- Mark the test using the Reading Mark Scheme provided on CD-ROM.
- Add together the marks from both parts of the reading tests (possible total of 30 marks).
- Use the levelling grid at the end of the Mark Scheme to level the test.
- When awarding an end-of-year Teacher Assessment Level, you will need to consider a child's performance during Periodic and Day-to-Day Assessments. If a child has achieved level 3 or above in the transitional tests, it can be assumed that they have achieved AF1 at that level.

Writing tasks: instructions

There are two writing tasks provided at each level (levels 1–3) on the CD-ROM. Each writing task is divided into two parts: shorter and longer writing tasks.

Administering the tasks
Shorter writing task
Allow 15 minutes for each task at level 1, and 20 minutes at levels 2 and 3.
Longer writing task
Allow 25 minutes for each task at level 1, and 30 minutes at levels 2 and 3.
- Children should sit so that they cannot see each other's work.
- Read the task to the children; do not explain the task or help them.
- The task may be administered to groups of children or to the whole class.
- Do not allow children to use dictionaries or word books.

Equipment for each child:
Pencil, eraser (or children may cross out mistakes) and sheets of plain paper.

Introducing the writing tasks
At level 1, each task should be introduced to the children following the task guidelines. At levels 2 and 3 say to the children: *I am going to ask you to do some writing. I will read the task to you, but I cannot help you with your ideas. If you make a mistake, cross it out (or rub it out neatly) and write your word clearly. Spell the words as best you can, building them up as you usually do.*

Marking and levelling the children
- Mark each piece of writing separately using the Writing Mark Scheme, Table 1, provided on the CD-ROM.
- Double the marks gained for the longer Writing task and add this total to the mark gained for the shorter Writing task.
- Assess spelling and handwriting across both pieces of writing using Table 2, provided on the CD-ROM.
- Add the total gained from Table 1 to the total from Table 2.
- Use the grid at the end of the Mark Scheme to find a level for each child.